WHAT *is* RIGHT?

Biblical Principles for Decision-Making

ELMER TOWNS

DESTINY IMAGE® PUBLISHERS, INC.
P.O. Box 310, Shippensburg, PA 17257-0310
"Promoting Inspired Lives."

This book and all other Destiny Image and Destiny Image Fiction books are available at Christian bookstores and distributors worldwide.

Cover design by Eileen Rockwell

For more information on foreign distributors, call 717-532-3040.

Reach us on the Internet: www.destinyimage.com.

ISBN 13 TP: 978-0-7684-7604-0

ISBN 13 eBook: 978-0-7684-7605-7

For Worldwide Distribution.

1 2 3 4 5 6 7 8 / 28 27 26 25 24

TABLE OF CONTENTS

Part Three

Part Four

PART ONE

WHAT IS RIGHT?

INTRODUCTION

AMERICA is in the midst of a moral revolution. After a generation of being told there are no moral absolutes, people are beginning to question the wisdom of that presupposition. The new revolution in American society is beginning to recognize absolutes in different areas. Sometimes, these absolutes relate to political and/or economic principles. At other times they relate to issues of public safety. Individuals are also beginning to ask "What is right?" in matters of personal morality.

This book deals with areas of great concern to Christians today. It addresses several specific issues, in which Christians are asking, "What is right?" It is written with the presupposition that the Word of God tells us what is right.

The things that concern Christians today are often related to the body. Some of these things relate to our mouth, knowing what is right in the use of language. Others relate to our eyes, knowing what is right in videos, television, and movies. Still others relate to our ears, knowing what is right in music. Then there are issues which relate to our entire body, knowing what is right in dancing.

Other issues discussed in this book deal with larger social issues in society. The Bible has very specific things to say about America's largest drug problem, alcohol abuse. It also has much to say about another important social problem today, racism.

The purpose of this book is not to list right and wrong behavior, but rather communicate biblical principles you can use to help you determine what is right. When God made people, He made them rational, thinking beings in His image. That means each of us can apply biblical principles to situations facing us and determine what is the right thing to do or say. This book deals with principles rather than methods. The principles explained in each chapter are listed in the appendix at the end of this book for quick reference in your own decision-making.

Methods are many, principles are few. Methods may change, principles never do. May God help each of us consistently apply the principles of God's word to every situation and do what is right.

Elmer Towns

Lynchburg, Virginia

Chapter 1

PRESUPPOSITIONS AND PRINCIPLES

DECISION-MAKING is an integral part of our daily lives. We make choices about the foods we eat, the books and magazines we read, the music we listen to, and the places we go. Often, these decisions are based upon personal preferences at the time. When we go out to eat, the choice of restaurant depends largely upon whether we would rather eat pizza, tacos, Chinese food, chicken, steak, or fish, and so on. Our preference in foods may even change from meal to meal.

Other decisions we make are more complicated. These decisions involve more than personal preferences. They also involve moral and ethical considerations. The family and cultural values we have adopted as our own help us make these kinds of decisions. For Christians, Christian ethics and biblical principles are also involved in making ethical choices.

When we make an ethical choice, we may choose to do something different than our friends or family members may do. Each person makes his or her own ethical decision based upon his or her own unique presuppositions. Presuppositions are self-evident truths. They are the principles and means by which we determine what is right and wrong.

FOUNDATIONAL BIBLICAL PRESUPPOSITIONS

There are several foundational biblical presuppositions that are the basis for the ethical decisions we make. These self-evident truths guide us through the maze of determining the rightness and/or wrongness involved in our choices. They represent core values at the ethical center of our being.

The first of these presuppositions may be summarized in the statement, "God is the source of right." Adjectives like "truth" and "righteous" describe attributes so characteristic of God that they appear in various names and titles of each member of the Trinity. Our God is "the true God" who stands unique from all other contenders (Deut. 32:4). Jesus described Himself to His disciples declaring, "I am the way, the truth, and the life" (John 14:6). The Holy Spirit at work in our lives is called the "Spirit of Truth" (John 14:17). Even the word of God may be characterized by truth (John 17:17).

Our second presupposition is that the opposite of right is sin. The concept of sin is described in Scripture in several ways. According to the Bible, sin may be both active and passive. There are sins of commission and sins of omission. Just as certain activities may be *wrong*, not engaging in *right* behavior may also be described as sin. Also, sin may be known or unknown. In our courts, a plea of ignorance of the law is not an acceptable excuse. In comparison, ignorance does not exempt us from moral responsibility in the area of sin.

People develop their own concepts of sin based on the moral values at work in their society. As the end of the twentieth century approaches, one of the core values of American society is that of good health. Our society believes in "survival-of-the-fittest" and is opposed to that which may be harmful to the health and well being of others. Lobby groups that understand this core value in American society have begun to change American behavior by appealing to their core value of health and well-being. Although churches preached against behavior like smoking and drinking, real social change was not affected until these groups appealed to the social conscience of Americans. Today, smoking in public places and driving under the influence of alcohol are strongly opposed in many American cities. As a result, these new laws are changing American behavior in a way the sin taxes never did. Christians concerned about other social and moral problems like homosexuality and abortion may not be able to change society until they can demonstrate how these activities impact our quality of life in a negative way.

Our third presupposition concerns God's motives in calling for ethical behavior. The motive of right behavior and attitudes is love. God cannot make principles to harm me. Nor can He cause principles to mislead me. He is, by nature, "a rewarder" who is more interested in our welfare than we are ourselves (Heb. 11:6). Therefore, God will not introduce principles to withhold me from that which is good. He does reserve the right to allow circumstances, His laws, and various trials to become part of our experience to mold us into the image of His Son (Rom. 8:28, 29).

The purpose of right attitudes and behavior is to glorify God. The first question asked in the *Westminster Shorter Catechism* is, "What is the chief end of man?" The correct answer to that question is, "Man's chief end is to glorify God and to enjoy Him for ever." Doing and being right is not an end in itself, but rather a means by which we accomplish the end of glorifying God.

Sometimes people talk about certain crimes as "victimless crimes," meaning that although the behavior is regarded as illegal, no one is really hurt by them. In light of our purpose in life, the concept of a victimless crime is a misnomer. An activity like cursing may be viewed as a victimless crime by many, but cursing offends God who should be glorified. If the purpose of right is to glorify God, there is no victimless crime.

Fifth, the priority of right is people. God does what He does for people. The eighth psalm asks the question, "What is man?" (Ps. 8:4). The answer is that people are created beings, created in the image of God (Gen. 1:26). Even after the fall of the human race, people retained that image of God. Violence against people is viewed by God as violence against God Himself (Gen. 9:6). When we understand this principle, it becomes obvious that people are God's representatives on this earth.

A sixth basic biblical presupposition is the assurance that one can know what is right. God did not make people to be a tin soldier or sculpture. Rather, He made us with the intellectual capacity to think, analyze, and reason. Nor did God make us like an android, programmed to respond in a predetermined manner. God has also given us a will. This is a self-evident truth confirmed in the experience of every parent. They know experientially that even a two-year old can think and has a will. People are made in the image of God with personalities that allow us to think and respond independently.

God sustains this world by establishing specific principles by which it is governed. These principles of God are self-evident. We can know things to the degree that we can observe. All mankind is given some power of thinking and knowing. We accept the logical and reject the illogical.

BIBLICAL PRINCIPLES FOR MAKING ETHICAL DECISIONS

These basic presuppositions are expressed in a wide variety of biblical principles for making ethical decisions. The appendix summarizes many of the principles reviewed throughout this book. These various principles have specific application in different situations in which we find ourselves. In light of the presuppositions discussed above, there are eight biblical principles which provide a general guide for making ethical decisions.

The first of these principles may be described as the principle of obeying light. This means we must be ready to obey that which has been clearly revealed to us as correct in attitudes and behavior. The Bible teaches, "The secret things belong to the Lord our God, but those things which are revealed belong to us and to our children forever, that we may do all the words of this law (Deut. 29:29). This principle may be illustrated in the problem of taking God's name in vain. One of the Ten Commandments is expressed,

"You shall not take the name of the Lord your God in vain, for the Lord will not hold him guiltless who takes His name in vain" (Ex. 20:7). This biblical statement, and others like it, make very clear God's attitude toward using His name in vain. God expects us to obey the light He has given us.

A second biblical principle involved in making ethical decisions is the principle of following rules. This principle was expressed to Joshua when he was directed to "observe to do according to all that is written in it" (i.e., the law) (Josh. 1:8). Joshua was directed to obey the rules he learned through meditating on the Scripture. A specific illustration of this principle is apparent in Paul's advice to the Corinthians concerning sexual immorality. He asked, "Or do you not know that your body is the temple of the Holy Spirit, who is in you, whom you have from God, and you are not your own? For you were bought at a price; therefore glorify God in your body and in your spirit, which are God's" (1 Cor. 6:20). Because our body is the temple of the Holy Spirit, we are to glorify God in our body and not engage in activities which are harmful to the body.

A third biblical principle is the principle of clear thoughts. This principle recognizes that sin may be expressed as an attitude long before it is expressed as an action (James 1:14,15). The principle of clear thoughts is at the heart of the tenth commandment. "You shall not covet your neighbor's house; you shall not covet your neighbor's wife, nor his manservant, nor his maidservant, nor his ox, nor his donkey, nor anything that is your neighbor's" (Ex. 20:17). Jesus applied this principle throughout His Sermon on the Mount when He contrasted murder with anger (Matt. 5:21, 22) and adultery with lust (Matt. 5:27, 28).

A fourth biblical principle that should be applied in making ethical decisions is the principle of respecting others. This principle is implied in the first question ever asked of God.

"Am I, my brother's keeper?" (Gen. 4:9). The teaching of Scripture is a resounding yes.

Throughout the New Testament, this principle is emphasized in the various responsibilities Christians have to one another. Paul applied this principle when he counseled the Corinthians concerning eating meat offered to idols. Even though Christians might have liberty to do so, Paul cautioned, "But beware lest somehow this liberty of yours becomes a stumbling block to those who are weak" (1 Cor. 8:9). He reminded them, "But when you thus sin against the brethren, and wound their weak conscience, you sin against Christ" (1 Cor. 8:12).

A fifth principle to consider in making ethical decisions is that of following Christ's example. This principle was stated by Peter in his advice to Christians concerning how to respond to suffering. "For to this you were called, because Christ also suffered for us, leaving us an example, that you should follow His steps" (1 Pet. 2:21). In his classic, *In His Steps*, Charles Sheldon tells the story of a church and community that was transformed by asking the question, "What would Jesus do?" to guide them in their decision making. Although Sheldon's story was a fictional account, adopting this principle in real life makes good sense.

A sixth principle in making ethical decisions is the principle of following your conscience. God has given us a conscience to help us discern right from wrong. Paul explained this principle when he observed, "for down in their hearts they know right from wrong. God's laws are written within them; their own conscience accuses them, or sometimes excuses them" (Rom. 2:15, LB). Sometimes this principle is expressed in the popular statement, "If in doubt, don't!"

Closely related to this principle is the principle of internal integrity. If you think an activity is wrong and you do it, that activity is wrong for you whether it is wrong for others or not. Paul also expressed this principle in his Epistle to the Romans. "But anyone who believes that something he wants to do is wrong shouldn't do it. He sins if he does, for he thinks it is wrong, and so for him it is wrong. Anything that is done apart from what he feels is right is sin (Rom. 14:23).

The eighth principle involved in making ethical decisions is the principle of physical integrity. Our commitment to Christ involves yielding our bodies to God (Rom. 12:1). Therefore, activities which are harmful to our bodies are wrong to engage in. Paul used this principle in urging Christians to avoid sexual immorality. "That is why I say to run from sexual sin. No other sin affects the body as this one does. When you sin this sin it is against your own body" (1 Cor. 6:18).

The Christian who is committed to glorifying God in every area of his or her life will be careful to make ethical decisions to help him or her live consistently. Various Christians may disagree over specific behavior or issues, but it is of utmost importance that each of us has a standard by which we live our life. As you seek to determine what is right in your life, be careful to apply these and other biblical principles to the issues you face.

DISCUSSION QUESTION

What happens to believers who don't have a biblical basis for separation?

Chapter 2

VIDEOS, MOVIES, AND TELEVISION

DURING the last half of the twentieth century, video media has become a dominant force in American society. In 1948, there were only a few thousand televisions in American homes. Four years later, there were 15 million. Today, the average American watches four to five hours of television daily. The average American family watches seven hours of television daily. It has become the most preferred leisure-time activity in the country.

With the growth in the popularity of television, there has also been an increase in the number of people watching movies. In the early days of the movie industry, people tended to watch a movie once. Today, it is not uncommon for people to repeatedly view the same movie.

As a result, movies have become more influential in society than they were in the past.

Aggressive advertisers commonly coordinate the theme of a major advertising campaign with the theme and/or characters of a major motion picture release. The popularity of new movies has given rise to a new industry, the home video market.

The influence of media is evident in the fads and trends of modern society. When Disney released the film, "Davy Crockett," the demand for raccoon skin hats became America's first fad. Hundreds have followed in the years since. Often, popular hairstyles, fashions, and expressions are those featured prominently in film. Even public values and opinions are being shaped by the video media today.

Indications are that television and the video media will continue to influence American culture in the immediate future. We find ourselves today in a period of transition. The traditional three-channel option provided by the major television networks is becoming obsolete. Satellite and cable technology now makes it possible to offer American homes over five hundred channel options. Specialty channels offering news, sports, weather, music, and video games are already in place in many cities.

WHERE IS AMERICA MOVING IN TELEVISION?

Over the years, television and the video media have changed focus from reflecting society to changing society. In the past, movies and television broadcasting were largely based on the perceived norms within the viewing audience. Andy Griffith was Opie's caring father. The Beaver was a normal child trying to figure out life. Even the Beverly Hillbillies were an extended family. Today the media is moving from reflecting society to changing social values. While doing research for this book, I asked several people, "What do you think is the major contribution of television and movies to American society?" Their answers were interesting. I was told television was a powerful entertainment media that can show positive values. When I asked these same people, "What do you think are the major negative influences of television and movies?" they told me the constant portrayal of sin and violence as norms tended to desensitize people to sin, introduce twisted values into the home and eat up family time.

PROBLEMS WITH THE MEDIA

The entertainment media has had its share of critics in recent years. Their evaluation of the media has identified a number of areas of concern. They confirm the incredible influence of the media in our life today and suggest this influence is not always being used in the best interest of society. One problem area with the media may be described as "learning problems." This problem identifies the role of the media in modeling. Children learn by mimicking the behavior they observe. When children spend long hours in front of the television, it tends to undermine their creativity. Also, the behavior they mimic tends to be destructive rather than positive. Further,

even though television communicates vast amounts of data, children are not assimilating what they hear and see. The learning that takes place tends to be dysfunctional.

Social problems are a second area of concern with the media. Programmers tend to use the media to communicate their social agenda. Eighty-nine percent of businessmen portrayed by the entertainment media are corrupt. Government officials are typically obtrusive. Professionals are portrayed as self-centered. Minorities tend to be guiltless victims. In a typical year, television portrays 1,400 sexual incidents. This kind of programming is eating away at the foundation of traditional American values.

The media also has a real problem with truth, accuracy, and fairness. It portrays a world that is not real. In television, about half of the people portrayed as living together are not married. According to the U.S. Census Bureau, only three percent of Americans have that kind of lifestyle. Seventy-five percent of television murders are by middle-age men, and 90 percent of murderers are white. In contrast, the Federal Bureau of Investigation reports that 60 percent of murders are committed by men under 30, and 47 percent of murderers are black. In television, Hispanics are involved in twice as many crimes as other groups, but crime records suggest they are really only involved in about 20 percent of crimes. Television programs also tend to favor women in feminist roles. Seventy percent of television women have feminist roles, and only seven percent are cast in traditional roles. Also, television consistently fails to show the consequences of violence.

Crime is a fourth problem area in the media. In recent years, the major problem of children under 15 has changed from theft to sex crimes. Comedian Flip Wilson made famous the line, "What you see is what you get." We are beginning to reap a harvest from the bad seed which has been sown in the media. Programs like *The Simpsons* tend to teach disrespect toward authorities. The increase in violence in television tends to desensitize people. I don't take the death of someone killed in a show seriously, but I may be bothered by a reported death in a news program.

The problem of violence in the media has long been recognized by many observers.

Violence in the movies targets the seven to 12-year-old male who is the main "moviegoer." Violent crimes in this demographic group are up 700 percent in recent years. Violence in children's programming like *The Mighty Morphin Power Rangers* is so extreme that broadcasters in Australia and Canada have chosen not to air that program despite its popularity.

There are also religious problems associated with the media. Typically, ministers are portrayed as ineffective do-gooders, immoral philanderers, and social misfits. Churches are portrayed as anti-progress, legalistic, archaic, and boring. When evangelicals objected strenuously to the release of the blasphemous film *The Last Temptation of Christ*, their concerns were largely ignored by the media.

HOW TO SOLVE THE MEDIA PROBLEM IN YOUR HOME!

While doing research for this book, I asked several people, "What are the rules in your household concerning movies and television?" Several positive suggestions were made. Some Christian families attended movies occasionally, but only after the values of the movie had been approved by the parents. Also, parents trained their children to turn off offensive commercials and walk out of a theater, or turn off the television or video if it became offensive. Parents also consulted the ratings system in making their decisions. A general rule of thumb was, "if you don't like it, don't watch it."

How should a Christian respond to the problem of the media? Ultimately, each person and family must make their own decisions about each specific situation. Christians that agree on other things may disagree on the media. As I survey the situation, there appears to be seven different approaches taken by Christians relating to the media.

Some Christians engage in consumer boycotts in hopes of getting advertisers to pressure the media into producing more acceptable entertainment. Commercial television networks and stations rely on advertising revenue to underwrite their expenses and make a profit. When customers refuse to buy a product because the company sponsors offensive programming, the company will often reconsider the decision to advertise during that program. When the funding is withdrawn and the cost of producing the program is no longer underwritten, the program is usually dropped by stations and/or networks.

Many Christians make decisions about the media based on the rating system. This works best when parents explain to their children why only certain kinds of programming are acceptable in their home. Even when using the rating system, it is advisable to include other factors such as choice, morality, and harm. A G-rated movie may be about a subject in which you have no interest. Also, many "family videos" contain subtle humor or minced oaths which you may not want communicated in your home. Many comedies use slapstick humor which may be more violent than you want influencing your young children.

A third approach may be described as the educational approach. When watching television or a video together as a family, it is advisable to take time to discuss what has just been seen. Parents can encourage children to follow the positive example of a hero and help other families by recommending the program or video to them. Also, take time to communicate the consequences of evil that may have been portrayed in the program.

A fourth approach to the media problem is to practice censorship. A parent may "censor" the videos that are purchased and/or rented in the home, but beyond the family unit itself, censorship raises a number of problems. Who should do the censoring? What standard should be used to evaluate programming? Christianity is always tolerant of others even though it is wrongly attacked for intolerance.

A fifth approach to this problem is to separate oneself from exposure to the media completely. A person does not have a problem choosing which movies are acceptable and unacceptable if he or she never goes to the theater. In 1954, the then president of Moody Bible Institute advised Christians they should not own a television set. He argued that the god of this world controlled the airwaves; therefore, Christians should not participate in that media.

Scripture teaches personal separation as a discipline of the Christian life. "Come out from among them and be separate says the Lord. Do not touch what is unclean, and I will receive you" (2 Cor. 6:17). When Christians are convinced that something is intrinsically evil, they have no choice but to separate themselves from it. Those who believe Christians should separate from the entertainment media argue that Christians have no right to assume entertainment will reflect our values. Instead of attempting to salvage what is perceived as not needed, they argue that Christians should support and enjoy the Christian arts and/or media.

For some people, stewardship becomes the primary issue in making media decisions. There are only 24 hours in a day, 168 hours in a week. This means decisions must be made on the basis of available time. Some people choose to limit their television time so they can engage in other activities which they value more.

Perhaps the most balanced approach to this problem may be summarized in the expression "immunization, but not isolation." Families which take this approach strive to teach their children Christian values without isolating them completely from the influence of the world around them. The idea is to teach Christian principles so children can filter out the positive values available in the media.

One of the most significant challenges you will face in your family relates to the television in the family rooms of the nation. May God help you and your family do what is right in the area of television and the entertainment media.

DISCUSSION QUESTION

How big is the problem of movies, videos, and television?

Chapter 3

MUSIC

THERE may be no area in which Christians disagree more than in the area of music. Each person has his or her own unique taste in music. To some, good music is always classical. To others, good music always has a country sound. Still others enjoy music that may be described as rock, rap, middle of the road, gospel, contemporary, or a host of other labels. Christians listen to, enjoy, and are edified by all of these kinds of music.

The problem is that Christians also find each of these musical styles offensive. Those who enjoy the opera do not usually get excited about attending *The Grand Old Opry* in Nashville. Those who find deep meaning and emotional expression in singing the great hymns of the church are sometimes uncomfortable with more contemporary praise choruses. The two most likely ministries in a church to be the center of controversy are the youth ministry and the music ministry. Sometimes both ministries become involved as people become concerned over the music sung by the youth group.

Perhaps the tension between Christians could be reduced if we understood the nature of music and knew why different people enjoy different kinds of music. In seeking to determine what is right in the area of music, it is important that we apply biblical principles to evaluate our music. Also, we need to understand there are some aspects of music that are neither immoral nor moral. Sometimes we like what we like because we like it. There is nothing wrong in that, but it can be very wrong to force others to adopt the same values in any area where there should be greater liberty.

VARIETIES OF CHURCH MUSIC

Scripture describes three aspects of church music. Paul told the Colossians, "Let the word of Christ dwell in you richly in all wisdom, teaching and admonishing one another in psalms and hymns and spiritual songs, singing with grace in your hearts to the Lord" (Col. 3:16). About the same time Paul wrote the Colossians, he also wrote an epistle to the Ephesians. On that occasion he called them to be filled with the Holy Spirit, "speaking to one another in psalms and hymns and spiritual songs, singing and making melody in your heart to the Lord" (Eph. 5:19). Each of these verses identify three aspects of music that may be sung privately or in the context of congregational singing.

The first of these aspects of church music is the singing of psalms. The book of Psalms has been described as the hymnbook of the Old Testament. A number of other portions of the Scripture in both the Old and New Testaments may have been originally written as hymns celebrating the greatness of our God. Throughout church history, Christians have sung the words of Scripture in a variety of ways. During the middle ages, much worship was limited to the Gregorian chants. Later, the singing of Scripture was prominent in the Scottish Psalter. Today, Scripture is sung in a variety of praise choruses reflecting several different musical styles.

The second aspect of church music identified by Paul is described as "hymns." This refers to the worship hymns which dominate the first part of many hymnbooks. These hymns help us focus on the character and attributes of God. This is reflected in titles like, *Holy, Holy, Holy, Great is Thy Faithfulness*, and *Majesty*. Each of these hymns, and thousands of others like them, cause us to reflect on specific aspects of God's character. As we meditate on who God is, our most natural response is to worship Him. The worship hymns in our hymnbook are effective tools in prompting and expressing our worship to God.

The third aspect of church music is described as "spiritual songs." This refers to the gospel or testimony songs that tend to dominate the later pages of our hymnbook. These songs tend to celebrate our relationship with God and His mighty works, especially as they relate to the Christian life. They include songs like, *Love Lifted Me, Since I Have Been Redeemed*, and *Heaven Came Down and Glory Filled My Soul*. These songs are important because they help us share our deepest experiences in the Christian life. They encourage both the singer and those who hear the song to continue enjoying their relationship with God.

Even though there are three aspects to church music, not all three are used in every church service. Rather, different churches tend to emphasize one aspect of church music more than others. Scripture tends to be sung by youth groups or traditional reformed churches. Worship songs tend to be more often sung in Presbyterian and pentecostal churches. Gospel or testimony songs characterize the singing one might expect in a Baptist or Methodist congregation.

FOUR PARTS TO MUSIC

Although there are three aspects to church music, there are many musical styles used by Christians today. In some churches, the use of musical instruments in worship services is restricted to some degree. Other churches may use a church orchestra. In the past, some church leaders opposed music in churches because it was viewed as immoral. Actually, music is amoral.

It may be used for good or evil purposes. It is what we do to music that makes it good or bad.

Before we can evaluate music, it is important to recognize that there are different parts to music. The first of these parts is the melody. Music begins with a melody. Melody refers to the dominant series of notes running through the song. Melody is usually tied to the words of a song and helps communicate its meaning.

The second part of music is harmony. Harmony is a simultaneous combination of tones, chorded structures as distinguished from melody and rhythm. Our emotions are affected by the harmony. When the harmony is written in major chords, the song helps us feel better. When the harmony is written in minor chords, the song tends to make us feel sadder.

The third part of music is rhythm. Every song has some rhythm. In some musical styles, rhythm is more dominant than in other styles. Some musical expressions such as rap are almost exclusively rhythm. Rhythm tends to affect us physically. It makes us want to move to the music.

The fourth part of a song is the words. Usually, the words and melody go together. The words of a song are the heart of the song. It is the message that is communicated in the song. Melody, harmony and rhythm relate to the words or message of the song. The music we enjoy most is that which is closest to our personal preference in music.

When asked, "What makes a good song?" my friend David Randlett uses a chicken as an illustration. In his illustration, the meat of the chicken is the melody, the barbecue sauce is harmony, and the salt is the rhythm. When you barbecue a chicken, the proper blend of chicken, sauce and salt is the key. Good taste makes good chicken and good music.

HOW TO TEST YOUR MUSIC?

We all have different preferences when it comes to the way we like our meat cooked. The same is true in the area of music. In these areas of preference we should exercise tolerance of one another. But there are other aspects of music that should be evaluated on the basis of relevant biblical principles. There are at least seven tests we can apply to determine what is right in the music we sing.

The first test is the message test. This test examines the words of the song to consider its message. Does this song express the will of God? If we seek to glorify God in all we do, it is important that the message of the songs we sing be consistent with the known and revealed will of God. Second, we need to apply the association test. No song exists in a vacuum. The association test asks the question, "Does the song identify with things, actions, or people that are contrary to Christianity?" An otherwise good song may be rejected because of its associations. Christians once objected to the singing of certain revival songs because they were written to popular melodies sung in British pubs.

The third test is the memory test. We tend to associate our memories and experiences with significant songs in our past. This can be positive or negative. The memory test asks, "Does the music bring back things in your past that you have left?" A song which may be enjoyed by some Christians should not be used by others who struggle with past memories.

The next test is the emotions test. Music stirs our emotions. Both negative and positive emotions can be stirred by music. The emotions tests asks, "Does the music stir the negative or lustful feelings within you?" This test causes us to evaluate how music affects us emotionally.

A fifth test to apply to our music is the purpose test. Music affects our emotions. Determine whether the music is sad, joyful, uplifting or soothing. Music which may be appropriate at one time may not be appropriate at another time. When we apply this test to our music, we choose songs which reflect our emotions or are Likely to produce the emotion we wish to feel.

The understanding test seeks to determine the meaning of the song. Should we use music that we don't understand or have a difficult time finding the melody? Some people enjoy and understand classical music. Others enjoy and understand country. Applying the understanding test, those who appreciate classical music would find it easier to worship God listening to a recording of Handle's Messiah than that of a gospel quartet. The quartet might help those who appreciate country music worship God better.

The final test may be described as the music test. Does the song have a song within it? The music test looks at the song to determine its merits based on the melody. It seeks to determine if the song is singable, if it flows comfortably from one line to another.

The history of church music suggests that every generation has its own music. Today, many Christians express their worship to God in praise and worship choruses.

May God help each of us find the right songs to use in our personal and corporate worship of God.

DISCUSSION QUESTION

How empty would our life be without any music?

Chapter 4

ALCOHOL

THE widespread use of alcohol in the United States has a significant effect on the quality of life in our country. Daily we hear reports of drunk driving, teenage drinking, and crimes of violence in which alcohol was involved. The problems associated with the alcohol industry has caused many people to ask the question, "Should alcohol products be banned from television advertising?"

The most significant drug problem in America is drinking alcoholic beverages. More people use and abuse alcohol than any other drug. The total cost of alcohol related crimes and health problems to America is estimated at 20 billion dollars a year. Some observers have suggested that if what is known about alcohol now was known during the prohibition, it is unlikely that prohibition would ever have been repealed.

Alcohol has a destructive effect in the lives of those who use it. During the Evangelical Revival, the Methodists used expressions like "finishing strong" and "dying well" to describe those who were faithful to the Lord to the end of their life. They recognized it was possible to start out strong in the Christian life but not finish strong. One biblical example of that is Noah. Before the flood, Noah preached against drinking, but after the flood he built a vineyard and became a drunk.

Alcohol also influences generations within a family. When a pregnant woman gets drunk, so does her baby. Alcohol in the woman's blood is passed on to a child. Researchers suggest this could give the children of alcoholics a physical predisposition to alcoholism. It is noteworthy that 52 percent of all alcoholics had alcoholic parents.

THE PROBLEM WITH ALCOHOL

Christians who oppose alcohol do so for several reasons. The first reason many Christians are opposed to drinking is because God rejects drunkenness. "And do not be drunk with wine, in which is dissipation; but be filled with the Spirit" (Eph. 5:18). The Christian life is to be lived in the fullness of the Holy Spirit rather than under the influence of alcohol. Drunkards are specifically identified in Scripture as individuals who will not "inherit the kingdom of God" (1 Cor. 6:10).

Long-term drunkenness has a destructive effect on the body. It is estimated about 30,000 Americans die annually from alcohol related physical disorders. The Christian is called upon to present his or her body to the Lord (Rom. 12:1). Also, the Bible teaches that the Christian's body is "the temple of the Holy Spirit" (1 Cor. 6:19). It is your Christian responsibility to "glorify God in your body" (1 Cor. 6:20).

Further, drunkenness destroys the morals and integrity of people. There is clearly a link between drunkenness and crime. This does not mean all who drink will commit crime. Rather, statistical research indicates most criminals drink excessively. Alcohol is directly involved in a significant number of crimes committed in America.

Drunkenness also destroys the self-control of people. People drink to "loosen up" and get rid of their inhibitions. Self-control is one aspect of the fruit of the Spirit (Gal. 5:23). The movement against drinking in the early part of this century was known as the Temperance Movement because it advocated self-control or temperance over drunkenness.

Drunkenness is contrary to the example of Christ. "For to this you were called, because Christ also suffered for us, leaving us an example, that you should follow in His steps" (1 Pet. 2:21). Five times the Bible claims that Jesus was without sin. Therefore, the Christian walking in the steps of Jesus will avoid the sin of drunkenness.

Alcohol is addictive. Those who become addicted to alcohol become compulsive in their thinking and behavior. No one is really certain why some people become addicted to alcohol faster than others. Many Christians avoid the use of alcohol completely, fearing that their first drink may be the one that begins a pattern of addiction in their life.

SHOULD A CHRISTIAN DRINK NON-ALCOHOLIC BEER?

In recent years, beer makers have begun promoting a "nonalcoholic" beer to consumers.

Actually, this product is only new in America. It has been available for years in other countries.

In Britain, beer drinkers differentiate between a large beer and a small beer. Small beers, or "non-alcoholic" beers, have less than one percent alcohol content in the brew (usually about half a percent).

When I was researching this chapter, I asked several people, "Should a Christian drink non-alcoholic beer?" The general consensus of those I asked was no. They argued this product was designed to encourage kids to drink and may prove to be a stepping stone to drinking stronger alcoholic beverages in the future.

When the Scriptures describe wine drinking, two different kinds of wine are mentioned. Strong wine was wine with an alcohol content. Good wine or new wine was similar to grape juice. Good wine was used in the worship of God and could be offered to God as a sacrifice. The difference between these two kinds of wine was fermentation.

Fermentation is the natural result of yeast growing in the brew. When wine makers age wine, they are allowing yeast to grow in the wine barrel. The byproduct of yeast in wine is alcohol. When the winemaker decides the wine has been brewed long enough, it is cooled and bottled. Cooling the wine kills the yeast and ends the fermentation process.

Yeast, or leaven, is prohibited in Scripture in any aspect of the worship of God. Bread used during religious feasts such as Passover was made without yeast.

Typically, yeast often represents sin. Six days before Passover each spring, Jewish homes are not allowed to have any leavened foods in them. The practice of "spring cleaning" has grown out of the efforts of Jewish women to cleanse their homes of leaven in preparation for Passover.

DID JESUS CONDONE DRINKING INTOXICATING WINE?

Sometimes it is argued that Jesus condoned drinking intoxicating wine. Generally, this claim is based on one or more of the three accounts where Jesus is linked to the drinking of wine. A closer look at each of these accounts will help us answer the question, "Did Jesus condone drinking intoxicating wine?"

The charge that Jesus drank intoxicating wine is sometimes based on Jesus' use of wine at the last supper with His disciples. The Greek terms used to describe good wine and strong wine are used interchangeably in the New Testament, so little help can be drawn from that source. However, there are strong arguments suggesting the wine used in the last supper was nonalcoholic. The first argument is the preparation argument. The observance of the last supper was a Passover meal, and leaven was strictly prohibited during the Passover season. Without leaven, wine cannot be fermented.

Two other arguments tend to reinforce the conclusion that Jesus drank non-alcoholic wine at the last supper. The command argument suggests Jesus would not violate a clear prohibition in Scripture. Habakkuk cried out to the people of his day, "Woe to him who gives drink to his neighbor, pressing him to your bottle, even to make him drunk that you may look on his nakedness!" (Hab. 2:15). A second argument, the implicit argument, notes the Scriptures never describe the beverage used at that meal as wine but rather "the fruit of the vine."

A second occasion sometimes cited to prove Jesus condoned the use of intoxicating wine is His first miracle, the changing of water into wine at the wedding in Cana. Once again, there are strong reasons for concluding the wine used on that occasion was not intoxicating wine. The social argument reminds us that the wedding was a family affair and it was customary not to serve intoxicating wine on such occasions. The process argument notes that Jesus accomplished this miracle by speeding up the natural process of transforming water into wine; therefore, the time needed for fermentation did not exist. Again, the command argument suggests Jesus would not violate the clear teaching of Scripture. "Do not look on the wine when it is red, when it sparkles in the cup, when it swirls around smoothly" (Prov. 23:31).

The third incident used to argue that Jesus condoned the use of intoxicating wine comes out of an accusation describing Jesus as "a winebibber" (Matt. 11:19; Luke 7:34). This charge needs to be understood in context. First, the charge came from enemies who called Him a devil (John 8:48). Also, the statement is made comparing Jesus' approach to life with that of John the Baptist, who was a Nazarite.

HOW TO BE SOBER LIFE-LONG

Sobriety is certainly a worthy goal for the Christian who is concerned about doing what is right in the area of consuming alcohol. The steps to' a life of sobriety begin with knowing right thinking. As noted above, strong drink is clearly prohibited in Scripture.

Second, learn to treat alcohol with respect. It is wise to be a little fearful about the effects and long-term consequences of alcohol use.

Next, follow the example of Christ. Jesus interacted with people in social situations without drinking alcoholic beverages. He was able to build relationships with the unsaved and convince them of His concern without splitting a six-pack with them. As we follow the example of Christ, we can also relate to others without using alcohol.

Fourth, make a commitment to your spouse to have an alcohol-free home. Alcohol has a destructive effect on family life, often leaving children struggling for years with problems associated with growing up in a dysfunctional family. Also, physical abuse in the home is often linked to drinking alcoholic beverages. Keeping alcohol out of your home will help you build a stronger family.

Promise yourself you will never take your first drink. If you have already used alcohol, promise yourself you will never take your next drink. Those who struggle with addiction to alcohol have learned the best way to deal with the problem is to not take the next drink. Be careful of alcohol-influenced attractions. This is especially important for those who struggle with an addiction to alcohol. When invited to a party, meeting, or event in which large amounts of alcohol are likely to be consumed, your best response is always to decline the invitation.

Finally, bend over backwards when in an alcoholic environment to avoid the appearance of evil. When John Diefenbaker was Prime Minister of Canada, his reputation as a "teetotaler" came under the close scrutiny of the press. Observers noted the Prime Minister always arranged to have soft drinks available on occasions where alcohol was likely to be consumed. On one occasion when a television reporter spiked the Prime Minister's drink, Deifenbaker held the glass the entire evening without taking a drink. Being forced into an alcoholic environment by his office, Prime Minister Diefenbaker took steps to insure he would not be viewed as one who participated in drinking alcoholic beverages.

Most of us will never face that kind of scrutiny in our lives. Still, we should be careful to avoid the appearance of evil and do that which is right when it comes to consuming alcoholic beverages.

DISCUSSION QUESTION

How can we communicate our beliefs about alcohol to others?

Chapter 5

LANGUAGE

ONE of the biggest struggles in the Christian life for many Christians is the tongue. James claimed, "For we all stumble in many things. If anyone does not stumble in word, he is a perfect man, able also to bridle the whole body" (James 3:2). He went on to add, "And the tongue is a fire, a world of iniquity. The tongue is so set among our members that it defiles the whole body, and sets on fire the course of nature; and it is set on fire by hell" (James 3:6). Then he lamented, "But no man can tame the tongue. It is an unruly evil, full of deadly poison" (James 3:8). The wrong use of language is usually the first indicator of a Christian who is falling from God. "Out of the same mouth proceed blessing and cursing" (James 3:10). This dysfunctional approach to speech is not compatible with the language that should be used by Christians. Paul told the Ephesians, "Let no corrupt communication proceed out of your mouth, but what is good for necessary edification, that it may impart grace to the hearers" (Eph. 4:29).

The wrong use of language is widely practiced in contemporary society. Those involved with people in a work or school setting are likely to hear language used that would not normally be used in church. Because we tend to become like those we associate with, it is easy to pick up language used at work or school and incorporate it unconsciously into our speech patterns.

VARIETIES OF CORRUPT COMMUNICATION

There are many expressions of corrupt communication or wrong language used by people today. These include swearing, cursing, blasphemy, filthy language, profanity, and slang. Each of these terms refers to a different aspect of wrong language.

Swearing involves uttering an oath or declaration with an appeal to God or a sacred object. When people swear, they are attempting to direct judgment or anger on people for mere emphasis.

Cursing involves asking God to bring harm or evil to a person or object. The result of cursing is to speak blasphemy. In Scripture, a curse carried its own power of execution. Cursing is the opposite of blessing.

Blasphemy involves directing curses or judgment toward God or His sacred object. The unpardonable sin, blasphemy against the Holy Spirit, involved attributing the obvious works of God to the devil.

Filthy Language is speech which may be described as morally vile. Often it is obscene or foul language with reference to parts of the body to convey the idea of disgust.

Profanity bridges the gap between swearing and filthy language. Its purpose is to show utter disregard for God.

Slang is language markedly colloquial. It is regarded as generally below the standards of cultural speech. Slang expressions are born into the common language of the people when a phrase is coined, having meaning to those within the "in group."

OBSERVATIONS FROM LIFE

As we look at society today, several observations become apparent. One of the most startling is in the apparent increase in swearing among women. Swearing is no longer dominated by men. In previous generations, swearing was looked upon as a manly thing to do, especially by young boys. Today, women are as likely to swear as men. This is one of the results of an equalization between the sexes which has been taking place in our society.

A second observation relates to frequency rates at which people swear. Swearing is no longer an occasional outburst in anger or frustration. Surveys reveal college students tend to swear at a rate of one

in fourteen words. These same studies suggest children swear at the same frequency rate as their parents. Swearing is becoming a significant part of the normal speech patterns of Americans.

The third observation relates to the legal arena. Organizations such as the American Civil Liberties Union represent people in court defending their right to swearing under the free speech provisions of the United States Constitution. These and other observations like them suggest the use of wrong language is becoming increasingly acceptable in society.

BIBLICAL OBSERVATIONS

The popular view of using wrong language is in conflict with biblical teaching on this issue. The third commandment clearly states, "You shall not take the name of the Lord your God in vain, for the Lord will not hold him guiltless who takes His name in vain" (Ex. 20:7). The Hebrew word translated "vain" in this commandment means waste, disorder, empty and includes using the name of the Lord in a lie. When God promises He "will not hold him guiltless," He is affirming those guilty of violating this command will not be allowed to go unpunished.

In the fuller statement of the law in Leviticus, the penalty for the crime of blasphemy was death by stoning. Following the death of Moses, there was a dispute over the body of Moses. Michael the archangel, even though he was contending with the devil, chose "not to bring against him a reviling accusation" (Jude 9). In contrast, Peter used cursing in his third denial of Christ.

The Scriptures consistently teach the Christian response to those who curse them. Jesus said, "Bless those who curse you" (Matt. 5:44). The Ephesians were instructed to speak "neither filthiness, nor foolish talking, nor coarse jesting, which are not fitting, but rather giving of thanks" (Eph. 5:4). Paul told the

Colossians, "But now is the time to cast off and throw away all these rotten garments of anger, hatred, cursing, and dirty language" (Col. 3:8, LB). Christians should not be guilty of using wrong language.

WHY DO PEOPLE USE WRONG LANGUAGE?

Studies have been done to determine why people use wrong language. These studies suggest several reasons for this behavior. Many people use wrong language to stir up authorities. Their swearing is an expression of rebellion against restraints. It is their way of expressing their desire for freedom or independence from those they view as oppressive.

A second reason why people swear is to express anger. When a worker hurts himself on the job, it is not uncommon for his first response to be an angry utterance of an oath or curse.

People may also be prompted to express their anger in swearing when injured emotionally.

Equalization is a third reason why people swear. This is especially true with women. Swearing has become a tool of feminism to make sexes equal. Being able to "swear like a man" is perceived by some feminists as a necessary step in achieving the goals of their movement.

A fourth reason some people swear is to flaunt superiority. In some circles, the ability to swear is valued as a mark of superiority. This is especially true in what would be generally viewed as negative and destructive subcultures.

For many, swearing has become a habit. These people may have begun swearing for other reasons, but they have sworn so much now that it has become an integral part of their normal speech pattern. Sometimes, habitual swearing is the result of years of following poor role models. When a child hears his parents habitually swearing, that language becomes a part of his or her speech pattern also.

The final reason people swear and use profane language is as an expression of their rebellion against God. When Jesus challenged the scribes and Pharisees of His day for placing their traditions above the clear teaching of Scripture, He reminded His listeners, "Not what goes into the mouth defiles a man; but what comes out of the mouth, this defiles a man" (Matt. 15:11). People who are angry with God and resisting His claim on their life often express that anger and rebellion in wrong language.

TWELVE STEPS TO PROPER SPEECH

In light of the biblical teaching on language, it is important that Christians seek to remove wrong language from their speech patterns and speak in a manner consistent with their Christian values. There are twelve steps that can help us deal with this problem.

To deal with the problem of wrong language, a believer must first realize his or her language is wrong. The decision to change one's speech patterns must be based on the conviction that the problem does exist in his or her life.

Next, Christians should be careful not to lead the way in changing bad words to good. Language is constantly changing and words that once had certain bad meanings may not have those meanings associated with them in the future. As society changes the meaning of words, it should not be Christians who are in the forefront of redeeming the language. If there is any doubt concerning words which may be in transition from bad to good, wait until there is no doubt the transition has been made before you use the word.

Third, try to be proper in all things. If the desire to do the right thing permeates every area of our lives, speaking the right thing will come easier. When we strive to use proper language, we will not find ourselves constantly struggling with questionable language.

Avoid using bad language to be accepted by the unchurched. While it is important to build relationships with the unchurched as a first step in reaching them for Christ, the use of wrong language may stall your efforts. Rather, as you build relationships with others, be careful to "let your light so shine before men, that they may see your good works and glorify your Father in heaven" (Matt. 5:16).

Fifth, realize wrong language interferes with growth and testimony. The key to the successful Christian life is to allow the life of Christ to live freely in your life. The use of wrong language places a barrier of sin between the Christian and the Lord, and hinders the Lord in accomplishing His will in that Christian's life. When this happens, sin should be confessed so our fellowship with God can once again be restored (1 John 1:9).

When Christians realize their speech is a reflection of their character and inner discipline, they will be more highly motivated to use correct language. That motivation will help them deal with inner disciplines and develop Christian character to help them overcome the habit of swearing.

In his Epistle to the Philippians, Paul wrote, "Finally, brethren, whatever things are true, whatever things are noble, whatever things are just, whatever things are pure, whatever things are lovely, whatever things are of good report, if there be any virtue and if there is anything praiseworthy - meditate on these things. The things which you learned and received and heard and saw in me, these do, and the God of peace will be with you" (Phil. 4:8,9). These verses identify two additional steps in dealing with the problem of language. First, stop watching unwholesome movies and exposing yourself to negative media. Second, pick out a Christian role model that does not have a problem in the area of language. When you have a question about using a word or expression, ask, "Would my role model use that language?"

A ninth step in dealing with wrong language is to get smart. Bad language is a dead giveaway of that person's ignorance. By building your vocabulary and expanding your learning, you will have greater resources to avoid using inappropriate language.

Don't separate yourself from people that curse, but be a testimony in their presence. As you bless those who curse you, they will be impressed by your consistent testimony. Replace evil speaking in your life by being "kind to one another, tender-hearted, forgiving one another, just as God in Christ also forgave you" (Eph. 4:32).

Be careful in all your speech. A good guideline is to "let your speech always be with grace, seasoned with salt, that you may know how you ought to answer each one" (Col. 4:6). Words are like a feather pillow shaken in the wind. It is impossible to collect all the feathers and take back words once they are spoken.

Finally, develop the discipline of memorizing and meditating on the Scriptures. "Let the word of Christ dwell in you richly in all wisdom, teaching, and admonishing one another in psalms and hymns and spiritual songs, singing with grace in your hearts to the Lord" (Col. 3:16). As you consider these twelve steps, may God help you also to speak what is right.

DISCUSSION QUESTIONS

Is language okay if we don't know it is wrong? How can we break the habit of using inappropriate words?

Chapter 6

SHOULD CHRISTIANS DANCE?

CHRISTIAN fathers and daughters have argued about dancing more than any other issue. This is especially true when fathers who are converted later in life discuss the subject with their daughters who are raised in the sheltered environment of an evangelical church. The issue quickly moves from a rational discussion to an emotional argument. Should Christians dance?

The dictionary defines dancing as a series of rhythmic and patterned bodily movements performed to music. This broad definition applies to many physical expressions to music other than what takes place at the Friday night dance in a local school. When the school band marches to music and when people clap to the rhythm of a gospel song, they are in the broadest sense of the word engaged in dancing.

To understand dancing, it is important to understand music and how it affects us (see chapter three). Music includes melody, harmony, and rhythm. The melody of a song is tied to the words or message. Harmony gives the song a broader sound, producing the feeling. Rhythm invokes the physical response. When someone dances to music, they are dancing to the rhythm of a song, not the melody or harmony.

As I was researching this chapter, several people drew my attention to the biblical account of David dancing before the Lord (2 Sam. 6:14). Biblical dancing was an emotional and physical expression of the entire body in rhythmic movement to music for a specific purpose. Before we accept David's example to justify attending the school prom, three questions should be considered. First, "What is your purpose in dancing?" David danced to God. Second, "What are you expressing in your dance?" David's dance was art expression of praise. Third, "How are you moving?" The Bible describes David as "leaping and whirling before the Lord" suggesting positive emotions such as joy and enthusiasm.

When I began researching this chapter, I assumed the Bible would forbid all forms of dance. That has been the historical view of evangelical Christians. As I looked up every reference to dancing in" Scripture, I was surprised to find there is no clear pattern forbidding all dancing. Instead, some dances appear acceptable while others are definitely wrong. To make a decision about dancing, it is important to understand why these dances were or were not acceptable.

A TIME TO REFRAIN FROM DANCING

Scripture describes two occasions when dancing was definitely wrong. The first of these is the Old Testament record of dancing before the golden calf at Mount Sinai. The second is the New Testament account of the dance of Herodias' daughter, which ended in the beheading of John the Baptist. Each of these incidents reveals a reason why dancing may be viewed as an unacceptable behavior.

The first negative example of dancing took place at Mount Sinai. "So it was, as soon as he came near the camp, that he saw the calf and the dancing. So Moses' anger became hot, and he cast the tablets out of his hands and broke them at the foot of the mountain" (Ex. 32:19). This dancing was an expression of the people's rebellion against God.

The second example of unacceptable dancing in the Bible took place in Herod's palace on his birthday. "And when Herodias' daughter herself came in and danced, and pleased Herod and those who sat with him, the king said to the girl, 'Ask me whatever you want, and I will give it to you'" (Mark 6:22). This rash promise by Herod resulted in the execution of John the Baptist. The purpose of this dance was that of seduction. When dancing expresses rebellion against God or attempts to seduce another person, it is clearly forbidden in Scripture.

A TIME TO DANCE

In contrast to the two occasions when dancing was definitely wrong, there appear to have been other times when dancing was an acceptable behavior. Just as unacceptable dancing was associated with negative values, acceptable dancing in the Bible is related to positive values.

There are at least four descriptions of acceptable dancing in Scripture.

First, dancing was an acceptable expression of praise in Scripture. "Let them praise His name with the dance" (Ps. 149:3). "Praise Him with the timbrel and dance" (Ps. 150:4). The worship of God in Scripture involved the whole body, not just the lips.

Dancing is also described as an acceptable expression in the normal cycle of life. Among the seasons of life, there is "a time to weep, and a time to laugh; a time to mourn, and a time to dance" (Eccl. 3:4). This reference does not tell us how to identify the right time to dance.

The dancing of children is also described in Scripture as an apparently acceptable behavior. Jesus described children calling out, "We played the flute for you, and you did not dance; we mourned to you and you did not lament" (Matt. 11:17). There is no indication in this context that the dancing of children in the marketplace was wrong.

Dancing is also described in Scripture as a symbol of happiness. "You have turned for me my mourning into dancing; You have put off my sackcloth and clothed me with gladness" (Ps. 30:11).

SEVEN WAYS TO JUDGE DANCING

If dancing was both acceptable and not acceptable in Scripture, how does a Christian determine what is right in this area? The acceptability or non acceptability of dancing in the Bible was related to other factors beyond the physical movements of the dance. By applying a series of tests to a proposed dance, Christians can make an intelligent decision concerning whether or not they should be involved in that dance.

The first test to be applied to dancing is the thought test. Paul wrote, "Finally, brethren, whatever things are true, whatever things are noble, whatever things are just, whatever things are pure, whatever things are lovely, whatever things are of good report, if there is any virtue and if there is anything praiseworthy - meditate on these things" (Phil. 4:8). When we apply the thought test to dancing, we ask ourselves, "Will this dance help me have the correct focus in my thought life?"

The second test is the message test. This test relates to both the song to which one is dancing and the dance itself. Are the words (message) of this song consistent with the values I want to influence my life? Also, dancing itself communicates a message. When we apply the message test, we also ask, "is the message of this dance that which I really want communicated?"

The third test to apply to dancing is the desire test. Sin begins with desire. "But each one is tempted when he is drawn away by his own desires and enticed. Then, when desire has conceived, it gives birth to sin; and sin, when it is full-grown, brings forth death" (James 1:14, 15). When we apply the desire test to a dance, there are several questions to be answered. What does this dance do to my desires? Does this dance arouse my lust toward my partner? Does this dance lower my resistance so I may do something else?

The fourth test for dancing is the association test. Even if there is nothing wrong with the dance itself, it may be wrong for a Christian to become involved in light of some association with the dance. A Christian who was heavily involved in dancing before his or her conversion may wish to avoid dancing because of the sinful lifestyle associated with it in his or her mind.

The place test is a fifth test to be applied to dancing. Christians should avoid dancing in places associated with drug deals, underage drinking, and other unethical activities. Our purpose in life is to bring glory to God (John 17:5). Therefore, we should avoid placing ourselves in situations or environments where we cannot bring glory to God.

The testimony test is another important test to be applied to dancing. Even though we may have liberty to engage in certain activities, we should avoid doing so if our testimony could in some way hinder others. Paul warned the Corinthians, "But beware lest somehow this liberty of yours becomes a stumbling block to those who are weak" (1 Cor. 8:9). When making a decision about dancing, consider those who are likely to follow your example.

The final test to be applied to dancing is the music test. This test examines the music to which one is dancing. This test grows out of the principle of barbecue chicken (see chapter three). When you look at the music, harmony, and rhythm of a song, is this song in good taste? The music test is also related to the message test. Is the message of this song something I should be celebrating in a dance?

Remember our definition of dancing? Dancing is a series of rhythmic and patterned physical movements to music. Some of those movements may be not only acceptable but, preferable on occasion. Others may be inappropriate behavior for the Christian. As you work through this issue in your own life, may God help you do what is right as you move, or don't move, to the music.

DISCUSSION QUESTION

It seems that everything we do to music is dancing, so what is a believer to do?

Chapter 7

LIES

DURING a series of executive seminars over an eight year period, James Kouzes and Barry Posner asked over 15,000 managers to identify those characteristics they most admired in a leader. The results were surprising. Eighty-seven percent of those surveyed said that honesty was the quality they looked for most in a leader. The business community in America is looking for honest leadership.

Similar conclusions have been reached by political scientists who have studied polls to determine why people voted for particular candidates. While some people cast their ballots along party lines or choose a candidate for his or her views on a particular issue, a vast number of voters make their decision on the perceived integrity of the candidate. If a candidate is perceived to be honest, the voters tend to be willing to give him or her an opportunity to represent them. If a candidate is perceived to be dishonest, voters will choose not to vote, or register their vote for someone else as a protest. The protest vote is increasingly becoming a factor in democratic elections.

There is a consensus in society today that integrity is a value to be appreciated in the lives of people. Unfortunately, many who value integrity attempt to produce the fruit without nurturing the root that produces that fruit. Telling the truth is not an isolated part of a personal lifestyle. People who tell the truth consistently are people of personal integrity. People who struggle in the area of lying are people who lack integrity at the core of their being.

Integrity is important to God. God affirmed our responsibility to tell the truth in the ninth commandment. "You shall not bear false witness against your neighbor" (Ex. 20:16). Those who engage in lying secure God's displeasure. Among the seven things God hates, both "a lying tongue" and "a false witness who speaks lies" are listed (Prov. 6:17, 19). Because integrity is important to God, it should also be important to us. This means the problem of lying should be addressed by each of us.

WHEN IS A LIE A LIE?

There are at least three ways a lie may be expressed or practiced. The first may be described as an active lie. This is what most people think about when they think about lying. The dictionary describes an active lie when it defines lying as "to make an untruthful statement with the intent to deceive." Saying things to create deception in others is lying.

A second expression of lying may be called a passive lie. Those who engage in passive lying sometimes attempt to justify themselves, noting they did not "say" anything untrue. They are correct in that affirmation, but that is the definition of an active lie. A passive lie attempts to create a false or misleading impression. When a person attempts to convince someone of an untruth without stating it, he or she is engaged in passive lying.

The third kind of lie is an inner lie. An inner lie involves tolerating internal compromise with what you know is right. When a person obviously believes an untruth about us and we do nothing to convince them otherwise, we are engaged in an inner lie. The real danger of an inner lie is that we lie to ourselves. If this practice continues, we may be successful in deceiving ourselves into believing that lie.

FOUR STEPS IN MAKING A LIE

The practice of lying involves a process by which lies are produced. This process involves four steps. The first step begins with the liar when he or she determines to create deceit.

Lies, like most sins, exist as attitudes before they exist as expressions. This is one reason why Jesus addressed the problem of attitudes when He discussed integrity in the Sermon on the Mount (Matt. 5:33-37).

Step two in the process of lying involves relaying dishonesty. In this step, the liar expresses an untruth in some manner. Lies may be spoken or written or expressed in some other way. As noted above, a lie may be expressed actively or passively.

Step three in this process is intending to misrepresent the truth about this situation. Liars know the truth but deliberately attempt to convince others differently. This intent to deceive is at the heart of lying.

The fourth step usually involved in lying is an attempt to avoid moral responsibility and cover up the lie. When a person tells a lie, he or she usually has to tell another lie to avoid being caught. One lie quickly becomes a series of lies.

SEVENTEEN TYPES OF LIES

Perhaps the real reason, so many people look for integrity in their leaders is related to the prevalence of lying in our society. People lie often in many different ways. Consider the following descriptions of seventeen types of lies. How many of these lies have you seen in recent weeks? How many of these lies have been expressed by you?

Perhaps the best known expression of lying is the "white lie." This lie expresses an untruth which is perceived good for both the liar and the victim of a lie.

Another common lie is the "political lie" or flattery. When a person complements on the attractiveness of a garment that they believe is unattractive, he or she is engaged in a political lie.

Gossip is another expression of lying. Gossip takes place when we tell what we know we shouldn't. Scripture describes the gossip or tale-bearer as one who reveals secrets.

A fourth kind of lie is the sinister lie. This involves passing on an untruth for an evil purpose. "An evil-doer gives heed to false lips; a liar listens eagerly to a spiteful tongue" (Prov. 17:4).

Perhaps the most commonly accepted form of lying is the "jovial lie." This involves lying in an obvious way, without malice as a joke. An example of a jovial lie is a lie about one's age.

A "half lie" involves telling the truth, but not the whole truth. In a half lie, one tells the truth with the intent of deceiving. When Abram went to Egypt with Sarai, he reported Sarai was his sister but failed to identify her as his wife. His half lie was told intending to deceive the Egyptians about their relationship.

Sometimes, an "excuse" may be offered as a lie. When a person uses an excuse, the reason given may or may not be true. Often an excuse is an attempt to misrepresent the truth concerning some failure on our part.

An eighth expression of lying is "hypocrisy." The Greek word translated "hypocrite" in the New Testament originally referred to the actors in a play who used masks and costumes to play the roles of others. This term came to be used widely of those who claim to be something they are not. The hypocrite attempts to deceive others into thinking they are someone different than they really are.

Some lies may be described as "justifying lies." These are lies people tell to justify their actions. Often, the purpose of a justifying lie is to convince others they would have adopted a similar behavior under the circumstances.

A similar kind of lie is the "face-saving lie." Sometimes people lie to avoid embarrassment. When Sarah was confronted with her laughing to herself when she heard the prophecy concerning her pregnancy, she immediately responded, "I didn't laugh." She lied to avoid the embarrassment of the moment.

Sometimes Christians use the expression "evangelistic lying" to describe the practice of stretching the truth. A pastor may exaggerate the size of his congregation or amount received in the offering. An evangelist may exaggerate the number of people responding to his invitations. In the early church, Ananias and Sapphira lost their lives when they attempted to stretch the truth about their generosity.

A twelfth expression of lying is the "propaganda lie." During times of military conflict, it is common for those involved to report different results after a battle. Each side tells only the facts which best suits their purpose. People also tell propaganda lies when they tell their account to make their position sound more reasonable.

"Advertising lies" are another common expression of lying in our society. Advertisers may use words like "virtually" as a legal disclaimer as they attempt to deceive others of the merits of their product. People also use advertising lies to deceive others.

"Cheating" is another form of lying. When a student cheats on a test, he or she is attempting to deceive the teacher. A common expression of cheating occurs each spring as people complete their income tax forms.

Scripture also identifies "demonic lies." These are dangerous lies which have their source in evil spirits. A society which rejects the light God has given them will exchange "the truth of God for the lie, and worship and serve the creature rather than the Creator;" (Rom. 1:25). Paul warned the Thessalonians of a time when "God will send them strong delusion, that they should believe the lie" (2 Thess. 2:11).

Sometimes the expression "putting a spin on the truth" is used to describe another form of lying. In this lie, people attempt to interpret the obvious facts of a situation in their favor. This often happens during election campaigns as politicians explain away negative pole results. A seventeenth expression of lying may be described as the "plausibility of denial."

Sometimes, people conspire to conceal their involvement by claiming they did not know what was happening around them. If it is likely to be believed, an individual or group may release an immediate statement denying knowledge of a situation and avoid being confronted about what they did know.

HOW TO BE A TRUTHFUL PERSON & OVERCOME THE HABIT OF LYING

With so many different ways to lie, it is easy to see why so many people practice lying and become enslaved by the habit of lying. One of the biblical descriptions of the devil is "liar," so we should not be surprised when the world system he controls is given over to lying. But one of the descriptions of God is "truth," so Christians should be careful to build integrity into their life. There are ten things we can do to overcome the habit of lying and become a truthful person.

The first thing we need to do is look to our standard. Jesus said, "I am the way, the truth, and the life. No one comes to the Father except through Me" (John 14:6). If we want to become truthful people, we must look to the example of Jesus and seek to imitate His character in our lives.

Next, learn, to recognize the source of lies. Jesus said, "You are of your father the devil, and the desires of your father you want to do. He was a murderer from the beginning, and does not stand in the truth, because there is not truth in him. When he speaks a lie, he speaks from his own resources, for he is a liar and the father of it" (John 8:44).

Third, admit your human nature is deceitful. Never forget that you were born with a sin nature. "What comes out of man, that defiles a man. For from within, out of the heart of men, proceed evil thoughts, adulteries, fornications, murders, thefts, covetousness, wickedness, deceit, licentiousness, an evil eye, blasphemy, pride, foolishness. All these evil things come from within and defile a man" (Mark 7:20-23).

When we recall our own sin nature, we should also recognize the ultimate consequence of lying. "But the cowardly, unbelieving, abominable, murderers, sexually immoral, sorcerers, idolaters, and all liars shall have their part in the lake which burns with fire and brimstone, which is the second death" (Rev. 21:8).

Fifth, if you want to overcome lying you must adopt the lie-busting strategy proposed by Paul to the Ephesians. "Therefore, putting away lying, each one speak truth with his neighbor, for we are members of one another" (Eph. 4:25). We will only overcome lying in our life when we fulfill our Christian obligation of telling the truth to others.

Next, determine to be a radical disciple. This means allowing discipleship to reach down to the root of your being. Jesus described radical discipleship when He said, "If anyone desires to come after Me, let him deny himself, and take up his cross daily, and follow me" (Luke 9:23). Learn to walk in forgiveness rather than guilt. When Israel was guilty of lying to God,

"He, being full of compassion, forgave their iniquity and did not destroy them. Yes, many a time He turned His anger away, and did not stir up all His wrath" (Ps. 78:38). In the New Testament, we are reminded, "If we confess our sins, He is faithful and just to forgive us our sins and to cleanse us from all unrighteousness" (1 John 1:9).

God never intended for us to live the Christian life in our own strength. That is why it is important that we ask for the strength that is needed to overcome lying. That strength is found in Christ. "I can do all things through Christ who strengthens me" (Phil. 4:13).

Ninth, make a decision to tell the truth. There is a power in decision-making that helps one accomplish the desired goal. When you decide to be truthful and announce that decision to others, you are making yourself accountable to them. Knowing you are accountable to tell the truth will help you to tell the truth.

Finally, resolve to be a person of character. The liar compromises his or her character when lying. Eventually, the liar erodes all self-trust and self-worth he or she may have had.

Religious and financial compromise is also often involved when lying.

The world is looking for men and women of integrity today. The one people above all others that ought to practice integrity are Christians. May God help each of us to deal with the problem of lying and build integrity into our character.

DISCUSSION QUESTION

Are American Christians more truthful today than a generation ago?

Chapter 8

RACISM

FROM the streets of Los Angeles to the battle fields of Bosnia, racism is one of the world's most significant problems. When we think of racism, we often tend to think about its practice in a specific context such as the apartheid policies which have dominated much of the history of South Africa and of the attitude toward the Jews in Nazi Germany. Actually, racism is far more widely practiced. It is safe to say that this week, thousands of people around the world were denied basic human rights on the basis of their racial or ethnic background.

In its mildest form, racism is expressed in subtle ways which allow one race to dominate the popular culture in a multi-cultural society. At other times, it is expressed in words ranging from unfair ethnic jokes to offensive graffito spray painted on buildings in ethnic communities.

In many countries, members of certain ethnic groups are denied benefits and opportunities widely available to others. In its most extreme form, racism grows into genocide attempts as one gang seeks to destroy another or one tribe annihilates another. Many of the world's minor wars represent little more than extreme expressions of racism.

While much has been said throughout the years about people of different races living together in harmony, the theory has not been expressed in reality. Yugoslavia and Czechoslovakia are two of several nations which broke up in the nineties because significant ethnic groups within their borders determined they could no longer live in harmony. Numerous tribal disputes are threatening the national security of various African and Asian states.

WHERE DID RACES COME FROM?

The Greek and Hebrew words used to describe races in the Bible may be translated races, nations, or gentiles. The first mention of distinct ethnic groups in Scripture is found in the table of nations (Gen. 10:5). This listing of 70 different ethnic groups describes each one as descendants of a specific patriarch. Each of these nations grew out of an extended family over several generations. While some Bible teachers have argued this list of nations is complete, it is more likely 70 nations were mentioned specifically for their numerological significance. The number 70 was often used by the Jews to represent the whole as in the 70-member Sanhedrin which represented the whole of Israel. Moses also identified at least one additional "nation" two chapters later when he recorded the call of Abram (Gen. 12:2).

The summary of nations in Genesis 10 makes it clear that all nations are direct descendants of a common ancestor. Scripture reaffirms this truth in other places where Adam is seen as the biological source of the human race (Rom. 5:12). If we are all descendants of Adam through the line of Noah, why are different racial characteristics apparent? At least possible answers have been proposed by Bible teachers to address this question.

Some Bible teachers believe God created the races just as He also created Adam: The name Adam means "red man," suggesting that he may have had an appearance similar to that of the native people of North America. Those who hold this view suggest specific racial characteristics may have been assigned by God to the descendants of Noah. One expression of this view argues that a darker skin color was part of a curse placed upon Canaan (Gen. 9:25).

A second view attributes racial characteristics to environment. This theory holds that racial characteristics tend to be adaptations over generations to environmental conditions. According to this view,

the darker skin people of Africa had prolonged exposure to the sun and the long winters of Scandinavia resulted in a paler skin color for that people.

A third view argues that all the races were created in Adam and that distinctive racial characteristics existed embryonically in Adam. According to this view, various specific racial characteristics became more prominent as a result of generations of inbreeding within one's ethnic group as the tribal nations became separated after the confusion of languages at Babel. This third view is also consistent with genetic research which has identified racial characteristics such as skin color and a predisposition to disease in some races to genes transmitted from generation to generation in DNA.

A THEOLOGY OF THE RACES

Although the Bible does propose a specific model for understanding the origin of the races, it does make it clear that God Himself is the source of these racial distinctions. God has made us all different. "When the Most High divided their inheritance to the nations, when He separated the sons of Adam, He set the boundaries of the peoples according to the number of the children of Israel" (Deut. 32:8). This verse suggests every race is in some way related to the Jewish people. This is interesting in light of the wide expression of anti-Semitism in a world in rebellion against God. How odd of God to choose the Jews.

Some ancient texts and translations of Deuteronomy 32:8 conclude the verse with a reference to the sons of God, i.e., angels (cf. LXX; NIV). If that reading is accurate, nations are in some way related to angels. Perhaps each nation has its own guardian angel. In both readings and views, God is the One separating the races. Whether He did it with reference to angels or Jews, God is the source of each race.

When God made Adam, He created him in "the image of God" (Gen. 1:26). This expression does not relate to physical appearance but rather personality. God does not have a physical body but is spirit. When God made man in His image, He gave people an intellect, emotions, and will. When we look at human personality, we gain insight into the personality of God. We understand God better when we look broadly at the various races.

God cannot be limited to a specific race or ethnic group. Instead, traces of the personality of God can be found in every race. Dominant traits in an ethnic personality are often the brunt of ethnic jokes or other unfair caricatures. Instead, we should see in the strong dominant will of the German, the excitement of the Italian, the entrepreneurial spirit of the Anglo, the hospitality of the Egyptian, the exuberant joy of the Latino, and self-discipline of the Oriental insights into what God is like. Just as light passing through a prism separates into a rainbow of colors, so God has expressed Himself to us through the prism of race. Since these racial characteristics are expressions of the personality of God Himself, attacks against another race represent an attack against God. It is a sin to be prejudice against another race or ethnic group.

God loves people of all races. Jesus came to die for people of all races (John 3:16). In His commission to the church, Jesus directed us to plant churches for all races (Matt. 28:19). God is not willing any should perish (2 Pet. 3:9). Rather, it is the will of God for all races to experience salvation (1 Tim. 2:4).

Scripture suggests that our racial characteristics will accompany us throughout eternity. John saw the elders in heaven singing, "You are worthy to take the scroll, and to open its seals; for You were slain, and have redeemed us to God by Your blood out of every tribe and tongue and people and nation" (Rev. 5:9). In describing those converted through the witness of the 144,000 Hebrew evangelists, John wrote, "After these things I looked, and behold, a great multitude which no one could number, of all nations, tribes, peoples, and tongues, standing before the throne and before the Lamb" (Rev. 7:9). He also described a river in the eternal city which was lined with trees whose leaves "were for the healing of the nations" (Rev. 22:2).

FIVE STEPS TOWARD RACISM

In light of the biblical teaching about races and God's attitude towards races, the practice of racism is something that should be avoided by Christians. Unfortunately, many Christians struggle with racism. One reason they may find it difficult to dispose of racial attitudes is because they fail to understand the steps one takes on his or her way to becoming a racist.

The first step toward racism is inward. People begin this process when they tend to value their race as superior based on racial differences to another. They begin to think they are better simply because they belong to a specific group. Ethnic pride may quickly degenerate into racial attitudes.

This is followed by a second step which is more outward. Those who begin viewing themselves as belonging to a better quality race soon begin devaluing other people belonging to other races. In their minds, these people are second or third class. This evaluation is made, not on the basis of any specific knowledge about the individual being devalued, but simply because he or she is a member of a visible minority.

Expression is the third step toward racism. At this point, the racist begins expressing outward actions to people of other racial and/or ethnic groups. These expressions may range from simple verbal insults to serious criminal actions taken against members of another race, including crimes of violence such as murder, assault, and rape.

These actions produce results that are detrimental to the offended race. Actually, the negative results of racism spread beyond the race attacked. The racist and his or her race also suffers the negative consequences of racism. Expressed prejudice leads to a segregation of the races. This means each race misses out on the contributions of other races to their quality of life.

The ultimate step in the racist path is a compromise in one's relationship with God. God instituted severe penalties for crimes against humanity because such crimes attacked one made in the image of God (Gen. 9:6). This suggests that God is offended when people are attacked. The individual with a racist attitude toward people of other ethnic backgrounds is offensive to God, who made that nation to reflect some special aspect of His personality. An attack on a race is an attack on God.

WHY DO PEOPLE TEND TO BE MORE RACIST TODAY?

Without question, race relations are disintegrating around the world today. Why do people tend to be more racist today than in previous generations? Several factors contribute to this problem. Race relations prosper when laws are applied equally to all races, but as America moves from a nation governed by law to a nation governed by precedent, members of visible minorities tend not to experience the same justice as people of other races.

Laws are an important factor in dealing with racism. Laws tend to subdue ancient hatreds, preventing them from being expressed in violence against others. This has become evident in the breakup of Yugoslavia. While there was much to be criticized in the oppressive communist regime that governed

that nation previously, the enforcement of law gave that society stability and Serbs and Moslems lived in harmony. As the nation broke up, the absence of law allowed old animosities to flair up into a devastating ethnic civil war.

The decline of Christianity is another factor contributing to the increase in racism. The principles of Christianity are inconsistent with the practice of racism. While it is true Christians have been racist in the past, those who practice their beliefs consistently embrace others of different races and seek to reach them for Christ.

The media also has a role in racism. In an effort to get a better rating, incidents involving racism tend to be given more coverage than might otherwise be given to the incident. Also, racism is a common theme in the entertainment media.

Sinful human attitudes like pride and ignorance also contribute to the problem of racism. In World War II, the holocaust and internment of Japanese people living in North America were violent expressions of racism. Today, ethnic cleansings around the world and politically correct language is used to minimize racial attitudes.

WHAT IS THE ANSWER TO RACISM?

When one recognizes God as the Creator of the races, the practice of racism is totally inconsistent with Christianity. Unfortunately, cultural values have influenced many of us, so we struggle with attitudes toward visible minorities in general or a particular ethnic group. There are some things we can do to deal with the problem of racism at a very personal level.

First, remember the mark by which Christians are to be identified, that of loving one another. On the night in which He was betrayed, Jesus left His disciples with a new commandment and noted, "By this all will know that you are My disciples, if you have love for one another" (John 13:35). The importance of that "new commandment" is emphasized as it is repeated twelve times in the New Testament.

Next, follow the example of Christ. Jesus was no doubt aware of the cultural attitudes of His people concerning the Samaritans, but He overcame those values to communicate the gospel with members of that ethnic group. When Jesus talked with the Samaritan woman, the significance of His actions were not lost. She asked, "How is it that You, being a Jew, ask a drink from me, a Samaritan woman?" (John 4:9). Throughout that conversation, Jesus avoided engaging in the issues that divided Jews and Samaritans as He built bridges to reach a woman and a city.

Cross-cultural evangelism as practiced by Jesus on that occasion should be part of the norm in our Christian experience. Jesus gave His followers a commission to "make disciples of all ethnic groups" (Matt. 28:19, ELT). It is impossible to fulfill the great commission without cross-cultural evangelism.

The gospel which saves people of our race or ethnic background is effective in saving people of other races and ethnic backgrounds. This was a difficult principle for the early Christians to grasp. When reports of Philip's ministry among the Samaritans reached the church in Jerusalem, a delegation was sent to determine what was happening. Later, when God brought salvation to Cornelius and his network of friends and relatives, Peter was very reluctant to cooperate. Later, he found himself defending his actions to other Jewish Christians who struggled with the conversion of non-Jews.

Perhaps we could overcome racism if we considered the new position all of us have in

Christ. In Christ, "there is neither Greek nor Jew, circumcised nor uncircumcised, barbarian, Scythian, slave nor free, but Christ is all and in all" (Col. 3:11; cf. Gal. 3:28).

There are some practical actions we can take to overcome racial attitudes. Begin giving to others, demanding nothing in return. Racial tensions are inflamed in a community when one group goes after special privileges denied to others. All of us can find people who are better off than we are, but take time to consider an ethnic group less fortunate than the one to which you belong.

Ask God for color-blind eyes. Learn to see people as individual human beings rather than members of a particular visible minority. We are all "one blood," having the same human characteristics. May God help us to live together in harmony with all the people of the world.

DISCUSSION QUESTION

What is the biggest racial problem or racial issue facing the church today?

Appendix

FOUNDATIONAL LAWS OF SEPARATION

THE following summarizes 27 foundational laws or principles of separation applied throughout this book. These biblical principles are useful in helping us make ethical decisions about the rightness or wrongness of our involvement in a wide variety of activities. Not every principle will be applicable in every situation, but it is anticipated that some principles in this list are applicable to each situation you are likely to encounter. The list is provided at the conclusion of this book to help you determine "what is right" in situations you encounter in life which are not specifically covered in the previous eight chapters.

1. The Principle of Addiction

   The principle of addiction states that a Christian should avoid any and all activity which might place him or her in bondage (1 Cor. 6:12).

2. The Principle of Appearances

   The principle of appearances states that a Christian should avoid the appearance of evil (1 Thess. 5:22).

3. The Principle of Association

   The principle of association states that a Christian should not associate closely to that which is incompatible to living the Christian life (1 Cor. 6:14).

4. The Principle of Barbecue Chicken

   The principle of barbecue chicken states that a Christian should have good and balanced taste in artistic matters (1 Cor. 12:31).

5. The Principle of Clear Thoughts

The principle of clear thoughts states that a Christian should have pure thoughts in his or her relationships with others (Matt. 5:28).

6. The Principle of Community Morals

The principle of community morals states that a Christian should live beyond commonly accepted moral standards in his or her community (1 Cor. 5:1).

7. The Principle of Consequences

The principle of consequences states that evil actions produce corrupt results (1 Cor. 15:33).

8. The Principle of Cultural Expectations

The principle of cultural expectations states that our Christian life should be expressed within our cultural world view (Rom. 2:14).

9. The Principle of Effect

The principle of effect states that Christians should consider the effect of an action upon them before engaging in that activity (Gal. 6:7).

10. The Principle of Financial Stewardship

The principle of financial stewardship reminds Christians that they are stewards of God's resources entrusted to them (Ps. 24:1).

11. The Principle of Following Christ's Example

The principle of following Christ's example states that Christians should pattern their lives after that of Christ (1 Peter 2:21).

12. The Principle of Following Your Conscience

The principle of following your conscience states that a Christian should never violate his or her conscience (Rom. 2:15).

13. The Principle of Following Rules

The principle of following rules states that a Christian should always obey the clear teaching of Scripture (Deut. 29:29).

14. The Principle of Incompatibility

The principle of incompatibility states that a Christian is radically different and, therefore, should avoid engaging in a partnership with another who does not share his or her values (2 Cor. 6:14-16).

15. The Principle of Intent

The principle of intent states that a Christian should question his or her motives in participating in a questionable activity (James 1:14, 15).

16. The Principle of Message Communicated

The principle of the message communicated states that a Christian should be careful to live in such a way that the message of his or her life causes others to glorify God (Matt. 5:18).

17. The Principle of Obeying Light

The principle of obeying light states that a Christian should act in accordance to the light he or she has on a matter (Acts 17:30).

18. The Principle of Personal Commitment

The principle of personal commitment states that a Christian should express decision in a commitment to someone else (Ruth 1:16, 17).

19. The Principle of Personal Integrity

The principle of personal integrity states that a Christian should avoid doing what he or she believes may be wrong whether it is wrong or not (Rom. 14:23). Sometimes this is expressed in the maxim, "If in doubt, don't."

20. The Principle of Physical Integrity

The principle of physical integrity states that a Christian should avoid activities which causes him or her to compromise their body (1 Cor. 6:18).

21. The Principle of the Place

The principle of the place states that a Christian should avoid places where he or she is unlikely to bring glory to God (John 17:5).

22. The Principle of Respecting Others

The principle of respecting others states that a Christian has a moral responsibility to be concerned for the welfare of others (1 Cor. 8:9, 12).

23. The Principle of Stewardship of Time

The principle of stewardship of time states that a Christian should make good use of the time available (Eph. 5:16).

24. The Principle of the Stumbling Block

The principle of the stumbling block states that a Christian should avoid any and all activities which might cause a weaker brother or sister to stumble in his or her Christian life (1 Cor. 8:9).

25. The Principle of Thinking

The principle of thinking states that the focus of a Christian's personal thought life should be compatible with the message of the gospel (Phil. 4:8).

26. The Principle of Ultimate Objective

The principle of ultimate objective states that the chief purpose of the Christian is to bring glory to God in all he or she does (1 Cor. 10:31).

27. The Principle of Values Education

The principle of values education states that Christian parents have a God-given responsibility to teach biblical principles to their children (Deut. 6:7-9).

May God bless you as you continue, in the midst of controversy, to do for Jesus, every day and in every way, what is right!

PART TWO

WHAT IS RIGHT?

Lessons

BIBLICAL PRINCIPLES FOR DECISION-MAKING

Presuppositions and Principles

A. INTRODUCTION

1. This series will deal with issues such as swearing, television, movies, music, dancing, pornography, alcohol, and stretching the truth.

2. Definition: Presupposition is a "self-evident truth" or the acceptance of a "cause" because it is proved by its effect. Synonym: premise, postulate, or basis. Principle is truth in application to life. Synonym: rule or standard.

B. BIBLICAL PRESUPPOSITION

1. The **source** of right: **God**. Since God is perfect, He cannot be wrong, nor can He direct anyone to a wrong attitude or action. Since God is all-powerful, all-knowing, all-everywhere present, He will direct everyone right.

2. The **opposite** of right: **sin**. If there is right, what is its opposite or its violation? Sin is an unpopular word. Our dictionary defines sin only with moral conditions and in relationship with God.

   a. Biblical view of sin is:

      i. **Active** and **passive**

      ii. **Commission** and **omission**

      iii. **Know** and **ignorant**

   b. Social view: failure, disaster, accident, or survival of the fittest.

3. The **motive** of right: **love**. "God is love" 1 John 4:8. Love is described as a positive and beneficial relationship by God for His people.

   a. He cannot make principles to **harm** us.

   b. He cannot cause principles to **mislead** us.

   c. He never will introduce principles to **withhold** good from us.

   d. He may allow circumstances to mature us.

4. The **purpose** of right: **to glorify God**. "The chief end of man is to glorify God and enjoy Him forever." Answer to first question. ~*Westminster Catechism*

5. The **priority** of right: **people**. God did not give principles just for Himself or nature, but for people. "What is man that You are mindful of him, for You have made him a little lower than the angels, and You have crowned him with glory and honor. You have made him to have dominion over the works of Your hands; You have put all *things* under his feet" (Ps. 8:4-6, NKJV).

6. The assurance of right: knowing. Christianity is a rational faith. "Come now let us reason together says the Lord" (Isa. 1:18, NKJV). We are made int eh image of God and got our mind from Him.

   a. His principles are "self-evident."

   b. We can know things to the degree we directly observe them.

   c. All mankind is given the same power of thinking, observing, and knowing.

   d. We accept that which is logical and reject that which is illogical.

   e. The world operates as a set of principles, i.e., physics (laws of nature), psychology, sociology, anthropology, logic, etc.

C. BIBLICAL PRINCIPLES

1. The principle of **obeying light**. Don't violate a clear scriptural command. "Thou shalt not take the name of the Lord thy God in vain" (Ex. 20:7).

2. The principle of **following rules**. Don't violate a clear scriptural principle. "Know ye not that your body is the temple of the Holy Spirit" (1 Cor. 6:19).

3. The principle of **clean thoughts**. Don't allow impure thoughts or deeds. "Whosoever looketh upon a woman to lust after her hath committed adultery with her already in his heart" (Matt. 5:28).

4. The principle of **respecting another person**. Don't harm another person. "Take heed lest by any means this liberty of yours becomes a stumbling block to them that are weak" (1 Cor. 8:9).

5. The principle of following **Christ's example**. Follow Christ's example. "Christ...leaving us an example, that ye should follow His steps" (1 Peter 2:21).

6. The principle of following your **conscience**. Don't violate your personal conscience. "God's laws are written within them; their own conscience accuses them; or sometimes excuses them" (Rom. 2:15, LB).

7. The principle of **internal integrity**. Don't harm your inner man. "Anyone who believes that something he wants to do is wrong shouldn't do it, he sins if he does, for he thinks it is wrong, and so for him it is wrong. Anything that is done apart from what he feels is right is sin" (Rom. 14:23, LB).

8. The principle of **physical integrity**. Don't harm your body. "Flee sexual sin. No other sin affects the body as this one does. When you sin this sin, it is against your own body" (1 Cor. 6:19, LB).

Lesson 1:

QUESTIONS

BIBLICAL PRINCIPLES FOR DECISION-MAKING

Presuppositions and Principles

A. INTRODUCTION

1. This series will deal with issues such as swearing, television, movies, music, dancing, pornography, alcohol, and stretching the truth.

2. Definition: Presupposition is a "self-evident truth" or the acceptance of a "cause" because it is proved by its effect. Synonym: premise, postulate, or basis. Principle is truth in application to life. Synonym: rule or standard.

B. BIBLICAL PRESUPPOSITION

1. The _____ of right: _____ . Since God is perfect, He cannot be wrong, nor can He direct anyone to a wrong attitude or action. Since God is all-powerful, all-knowing, all-everywhere present, He will direct everyone right.

2. The _____ of right: _____ . If there is right, what is its opposite or its violation? Sin is an unpopular word. Our dictionary defines sin only with moral conditions and in relationship with God.

   a. Biblical view of sin is:

      i. _____ and _____

      ii. _____ and _____

      iii. _____ and _____

   b. Social view: failure, disaster, accident, or survival of the fittest.

3. The _____ of right: _____ . "God is love" 1 John 4:8. Love is described as a positive and beneficial relationship by God for His people.

   a. He cannot make principles to _____ us.

   b. He cannot cause principles to _____ us.

   c. He never will introduce principles to _____ good from us.

   d. He may allow circumstances to mature us.

4. The _____ of right: _____ . "The chief end of man is to glorify God and enjoy Him forever." Answer to first question. —*Westminster Catechism*

5. The _____ of right: _____ . God did not give principles just for Himself or nature, but for people. "What is man that You are mindful of him, for You have made him a little lower than the angels, and You have crowned him with glory and honor. You have made him to have dominion over the works of Your hands; You have put all *things* under his feet" (Ps. 8:4-6, NKJV).

6. The assurance of right: knowing. Christianity is a rational faith. "Come now let us reason together says the Lord" (Isa. 1:18, NKJV). We are made int eh image of God and got our mind from Him.

   a. His principles are "self-evident."

   b. We can know things to the degree we directly observe them.

   c. All mankind is given the same power of thinking, observing, and knowing.

   d. We accept that which is logical and reject that which is illogical.

   e. The world operates as a set of principles, i.e., physics (laws of nature), psychology, sociology, anthropology, logic, etc.

C. BIBLICAL PRINCIPLES

1. The principle of _____ . Don't violate a clear scriptural command. "Thou shalt not take the name of the Lord thy God in vain" (Ex. 20:7).

2. The principle of _____ . Don't violate a clear scriptural principle. "Know ye not that your body is the temple of the Holy Spirit" (1 Cor. 6:19).

3. The principle of _____ . Don't allow impure thoughts or deeds. "Whosoever looketh upon a woman to lust after her hath committed adultery with her already in his heart" (Matt. 5:28).

4. The principle of _____ . Don't harm another person. "Take heed lest by any means this liberty of yours becomes a stumbling block to them that are weak" (1 Cor. 8:9).

5. The principle of following _____ . Follow Christ's example. "Christ...leaving us an example, that ye should follow His steps" (1 Peter 2:21).

6. The principle of following your _____ . Don't violate your personal conscience. "God's laws are written within them; their own conscience accuses them; or sometimes excuses them" (Rom. 2:15, LB).

7. The principle of _____ . Don't harm your inner man. "Anyone who believes that something he wants to do is wrong shouldn't do it, he sins if he does, for he thinks it is wrong, and so for him it is wrong. Anything that is done apart from what he feels is right is sin" (Rom. 14:23, LB).

8. The principle of _____ . Don't harm your body. "Flee sexual sin. No other sin affects the body as this one does. When you sin this sin, it is against your own body" (1 Cor. 6:19, LB).

Lesson 2:

VIDEOS, MOVIES, AND TELEVISION

A. INTRODUCTION

1. The average American watches television four to five hours a day, seven days a week per home.

2. Transition from three channels to over 900 channels.

3. From reflection of society to change society. From "Father Knows Best" to Madonna and erotic videos.

B. THE PROBLEMS OF THE MEDIA

1. Learning problems:

   a. **Modeling**. Children mimic the behavior observed: (1) undermines creativity (Lilian Katz, Ph.D., University of Illinois), (2) assumes destructive orientation to life, and (3) negative becomes greater than positive.

   b. **Communication** of data. Children see vastly more, yet do not interact with knowledge, understand it or apply it positively.

2. Social problems (research from Lichter, Lichter, and Rothman).

   a. Most businessmen and women are **corrupt or dishonest**.

   b. Most government **officials** are obstructive or manipulative.

   c. The sexual adventurer is a cool guy: 1,400 sexual instances each year.

   d. Professionals are sharing, selfness i.e., doctors, layers, journalists.

   e. **Minorities** are seen as guiltless victims.

   f. "Television is an acid eating away at the base of traditional society" (Lichter, Lichter, and Rothman).

3. Truth, accuracy, and fairness problems. Media does not look at both sides. It is not committed to "the truth, the whole truth, and nothing but the truth."

   a. Television shows 75% of murderers are **middle age** 90% by **whites** 60% under 30, and 47% are black (FBI).

   b. **Hispanics** commit twice as many crimes as any other minorities yet in actuality commit less than 20%.

   c. Television is bias to **feminist** roles, yet membership in non-feminist organizations is four times higher.

   d. The consequences of **violence** is not shown, (1) to the victim, (2) to the youthful criminal.

4. Crime problems:

   a. Fifteen years ago, the major crimes of children under 15 was theft, breaking and entering, and property crimes. Now it is **drug related crimes**.

   b. Television and movies teach **disrespect and rebellion** to authorities, i.e., police, social workers, judges, etc.

   c. Increase in violence **desensitized** people (1) to do it, and (2) what it does to people.

   d. "I don't take seriously someone begin killed on a show, but it bothers me on the news."

   e. Violence in movies targets the **12 to 17-year-old males** because they are the chief purchasers of movie tickets.

   f. Violent crimes by 12 to 17-year-old males are up 700% since 1962.

   g. Because of violence in American **cartoons**, the Canadian Broadcasting System will not show them.

   h. The rise in crime against women is in proportion to its rise in the media.

5. Religious problems:

   a. Ministers are portrayed as (1) ineffective "do-gooders," (2) immoral philanderers, and (3) social misfits.

   b. Churches are anti-progressive, legalistic, not enjoyable, and archaic.

   c. Ignored evangelical objections to **the last temptation of Christ** while media "buckles under" to objection by the NAACP, Jewish lobby, homosexual lobby, and the feminist lobby.

   d. Michael Medved, a Jewish co-host to Sneak Previews on PBS wrote *Hollywood vs. America*, Harper Collins, and documented movie's immoral and anti-God bias.

C. SOLUTIONS:

1. Consumer **pressure and boycott**. "Hollywood can clean up its act if enough consumers press for reform." ~Michael Medved.

2. Ratings system: God, PG, R, NC-7, X

   a. The **choice** factor.

   b. The **immoral** factor.

   c. The **harm** factor.

3. The **education** approach.

   a. Support and propagate **good** ones.

   b. Communicate the **harmful** effects of bad ones.

4. **Censorship** (determine what can be shown).

   a. Who will be the censors and who will appoint them?

   b. What will be the standards? 1800s? 1950s? 1980s? Protestant-Puritan ethic? The traditional American ethic?

   c. Christianity in the majority has unflinchingly held to one way of salvation yet is sympathetic and tolerant in ministering to everyone no matter what they believe. Yet when Christianity becomes a minority, it is attacked for **intolerance and bias**.

5. <u>Separation</u>. "Come out from them and be separate, says the Lord, touch no unclean thing, and I will receive you. I will be a Father to you, and you will be my sons and daughters says the Lord Almighty" (2 Cor. 6:17-18, NIV).

   a. Christianity has no right to assume entertainment will **reflect** their values, traditions, and faith.

   b. The Christian does not **need** worldly entertainment; there are other recreations.

   c. The Christian has his or her own art and music, he or she does not need to the world.

6. <u>Stewardship</u> of time, talent, and treasures. Christians have such a great calling; they shouldn't waste their resources on worldly media.

7. <u>Immunization</u>, not isolation. The believer cannot ignore the world (TV), in which he or she lives. In the world, but not of the world. "Not that you would take them out of the world but keep them from evil in the world" (John 17:15, NIV).

D. WARNINGS:

1. The world will <u>lull</u> us to sleep. Evangelicals are complacent about politics, community life, and entertainment.

2. The world <u>hates</u> us. "If the world hates you, ye know that it hated Me before it hated you."

3. The world will <u>harm</u> us. "Do not love the world or anything in the world. If anyone les the world, the love of the Father is not in him" (1 John 2:15).

4. The world will target our <u>children</u>. Rags to riches in three generations. —Richard Neibour.

VIDEOS, MOVIES, AND TELEVISION

A. INTRODUCTION

1. The average American watches television four to five hours a day, seven days a week per home.

2. Transition from three channels to over 900 channels.

3. From reflection of society to change society. From "Father Knows Best" to Madonna and erotic videos.

B. THE PROBLEMS OF THE MEDIA

1. Learning problems:

   a. _____ . Children mimic the behavior observed: (1) undermines creativity (Lilian Katz, Ph.D., University of Illinois), (2) assumes destructive orientation to life, and (3) negative becomes greater than positive.

   b. _____ of data. Children see vastly more, yet do not interact with knowledge, understand it or apply it positively.

2. Social problems (research from Lichter, Lichter, and Rothman).

   a. Most businessmen and women are _____ .

   b. Most government _____ are obstructive or manipulative.

   c. The sexual adventurer is a cool guy: 1,400 sexual instances each year.

   d. Professionals are sharing, selfness i.e., doctors, layers, journalists.

   e. _____ are seen as guiltless victims.

   f. "Television is an acid eating away at the base of traditional society" (Lichter, Lichter, and Rothman).

3. Truth, accuracy, and fairness problems. Media does not look at both sides. It is not committed to "the truth, the whole truth, and nothing but the truth."

   a. Television shows 75% of murderers are _____ 90% by _____ 60% under 30, and 47% are black (FBI).

   b. _____ commit twice as many crimes as any other minorities yet in actuality commit less than 20%.

   c. Television is bias to _____ roles, yet membership in non-feminist organizations is four times higher.

   d. The consequences of _____ is not shown, (1) to the victim, (2) to the youthful criminal.

4. Crime problems:

   a. Fifteen years ago, the major crimes of children under 15 was theft, breaking and entering, and property crimes. Now it is _____ .

   b. Television and movies teach _____ to authorities, i.e., police, social workers, judges, etc.

   c. Increase in violence _____ people (1) to do it, and (2) what it does to people.

   d. "I don't take seriously someone begin killed on a show, but it bothers me on the news."

   e. Violence in movies targets the _____ because they are the chief purchasers of movie tickets.

   f. Violent crimes by 12 to 17-year-old males are up 700% since 1962.

   g. Because of violence in American _____ , the Canadian Broadcasting System will not show them.

   h. The rise in crime against women is in proportion to its rise in the media.

5. Religious problems:

    a. Ministers are portrayed as (1) ineffective "do-gooders," (2) immoral philanderers, and (3) social misfits.

    b. Churches are anti-progressive, legalistic, not enjoyable, and archaic.

    c. Ignored evangelical objections to _____ while media "buckles under" to objection by the NAACP, Jewish lobby, homosexual lobby, and the feminist lobby.

    d. Michael Medved, a Jewish co-host to Sneak Previews on PBS wrote *Hollywood vs. America*, Harper Collins, and documented movie's immoral and anti-God bias.

C. SOLUTIONS:

1. Consumer _____ . "Hollywood can clean up its act if enough consumers press for reform." —Michael Medved.

2. Ratings system: God, PG, R, NC-7, X

    a. The _____ factor.

    b. The _____ factor.

    c. The _____ factor.

3. The _____ approach.

    a. Support and propagate _____ ones.

    b. Communicate the _____ effects of bad ones.

4. _____ (determine what can be shown).

    a. Who will be the censors and who will appoint them?

    b. What will be the standards? 1800s? 1950s? 1980s? Protestant-Puritan ethic? The traditional American ethic?

    c. Christianity in the majority has unflinchingly held to one way of salvation yet is sympathetic and tolerant in ministering to everyone no matter what they believe. Yet when Christianity becomes a minority, it is attacked for _____ .

5. _____ . "Come out from them and be separate, says the Lord, touch no unclean thing, and I will receive you. I will be a Father to you, and you will be my sons and daughters says the Lord Almighty" (2 Cor. 6:17-18, NIV).

   a. Christianity has no right to assume entertainment will _____ their values, traditions, and faith.

   b. The Christian does not _____ worldly entertainment; there are other recreations.

   c. The Christian has his or her own art and music, he or she does not need to the world.

6. _____ of time, talent, and treasures. Christians have such a great calling; they shouldn't waste their resources on worldly media.

7. _____ , not isolation. The believer cannot ignore the world (TV), in which he or she lives. In the world, but not of the world. "Not that you would take them out of the world but keep them from evil in the world" (John 17:15, NIV).

D. WARNINGS:

1. The world will _____ us to sleep. Evangelicals are complacent about politics, community life, and entertainment.

2. The world _____ us. "If the world hates you, ye know that it hated Me before it hated you."

3. The world will _____ us. "Do not love the world or anything in the world. If anyone les the world, the love of the Father is not in him" (1 John 2:15).

4. The world will target our _____ . Rags to riches in three generations. —Richard Neibour.

Lesson 3:

MUSIC

A. INTRODUCTION

Should a Christian listen to and enjoy all songs? When is a song inappropriate for the Christian? While music is amoral, i.e., neither good nor bad, it is usually the context of music that determines its moral nature. This lesson will help the believer determine what kind of music is appropriate for the Christian.

B. GOD'S PURPOSE FOR MUSIC

1. Three types of congregational music:

   a. **Scripture**.

   b. **Worship**.

   c. **Gospel**.

   "Teaching and admonishing one another in psalms and hymns and spiritual songs, singing with grace in your hearts to the Lord" (Col. 3:16).

2. Private music. "Speaking to one another in psalms and hymns and spiritual songs, singing and making melody in your heart to the Lord" (Eph. 5:19).

3. Who sings Scripture? **Youth and high church**.

4. Who sings worship? **Pentecostals and Presbyterians**.

5. Who sings gospel? **Baptist**.

C. WHAT IS MUSIC? (OXFORD DICTIONARY)

1. <u>Melody</u>. "Sounds in agreeable succession." The melody carries the words of the song.

2. <u>Harmony</u> (chords). "A simultaneous combination of tones, chorded structures as distinguished from melody and rhythm." Harmony effects the emotions or mood.

3. <u>Rhythm</u>. "Movement or procedure with uniform recurrence of a beat, accent, or pulse." Rhythm effects the physical. "David would take a harp and play it with his hand. Then Saul would become refreshed" (1 Sam. 16:23).

4. <u>Words</u>. The message that is communicated by the song.

D. TEST TO MEASURE YOUR MUSIC

1. The <u>message</u> test: Determine whether the message:

    a. Does it express the will of God?

    b. Is it neutral, i.e., reflective of normal life?

    c. Is it against Christian standards or behavior?

2. The <u>association</u> test: Does the music identify with things, actions, or people that are contrary to Christianity? "Come out from among them and be separate, says the Lord" (2 Cor. 6:17).

3. The <u>memory</u> test: Does the music bring back things in your past that you have left? "Forgetting the things which are behind" (Phil. 3:13).

4. The <u>emotions</u> test: Does the music stir negative or lustful feelings within you?

5. The <u>purpose</u> test: Determine whether the music is sad, joyful, uplifting, soothing, etc.

6. The <u>understanding</u> test: Should you use music you don't understand or to which you cannot find the melody? Sometimes you need music appreciation for the classics or cultural explanation for music from other cultures.

7. The <u>musical</u> test: Does it have the "song within the song?" It has meaning to you without analysis.

Lesson 3:

MUSIC

A. INTRODUCTION

Should a Christian listen to and enjoy all songs? When is a song inappropriate for the Christian? While music is amoral, i.e., neither good nor bad, it is usually the context of music that determines its moral nature. This lesson will help the believer determine what kind of music is appropriate for the Christian.

B. GOD'S PURPOSE FOR MUSIC

1. Three types of congregational music:

    a. _____ .

    b. _____ .

    c. _____ .

    "Teaching and admonishing one another in psalms and hymns and spiritual songs, singing with grace in your hearts to the Lord" (Col. 3:16).

2. Private music. "Speaking to one another in psalms and hymns and spiritual songs, singing and making melody in your heart to the Lord" (Eph. 5:19).

3. Who sings Scripture? _____ .

4. Who sings worship? _____ .

5. Who sings gospel? _____ .

C. WHAT IS MUSIC? (OXFORD DICTIONARY)

1. _____ . "Sounds in agreeable succession." The melody carries the words of the song.

2. _____ (chords). "A simultaneous combination of tones, chorded structures as distinguished from melody and rhythm." Harmony effects the emotions or mood.

3. _____ . "Movement or procedure with uniform recurrence of a beat, accent, or pulse." Rhythm effects the physical. "David would take a harp and play it with his hand. Then Saul would become refreshed" (1 Sam. 16:23).

4. _____ . The message that is communicated by the song.

D. TEST TO MEASURE YOUR MUSIC

1. The _____ test: Determine whether the message:

   a. Does it express the will of God?

   b. Is it neutral, i.e., reflective of normal life?

   c. Is it against Christian standards or behavior?

2. The _____ test: Does the music identify with things, actions, or people that are contrary to Christianity? "Come out from among them and be separate, says the Lord" (2 Cor. 6:17).

3. The _____ test: Does the music bring back things in your past that you have left? "Forgetting the things which are behind" (Phil. 3:13).

4. The _____ test: Does the music stir negative or lustful feelings within you?

5. The _____ test: Determine whether the music is sad, joyful, uplifting, soothing, etc.

6. The _____ test: Should you use music you don't understand or to which you cannot find the melody? Sometimes you need music appreciation for the classics or cultural explanation for music from other cultures.

7. The _____ test: Does it have the "song within the song?" It has meaning to you without analysis.

ALCOHOL: CAN WE DRINK?

A. INTRODUCTION

Should alcoholic products like tobacco products be banned from television advertisements?

1. **Alcohol** is the greatest drug problem, not crack, meth, marijuana, etc.

2. **Finish strong**. It is impossible for the young man to start right. "In the days of Noah, they were…eating and drinking" (Matt. 24:37-38). But later in life after the flood, "He (Noah) drank of the wine and was drunken" (Gen. 9:21).

3. When a pregnant woman gets drunk, so does her baby. Fifty-two percent of all alcoholics had **alcoholic parents**.

B. WHY I AM AGAINST LIQUOR

What are the primary reasons for not drinking alcohol products?

1. God **rejects** drunkenness. Be not drunk with wine wherein is excess but be filled with the Sprit" (Eph. 5:18). "Do not look on the wine when it is red, when it sparkles in the cup" (Prov. 23:31). "Their wine is the poison" (Deut. 32:33). "Woe to him who gives drink to his neighbor, pressing him to your bottle" (Hab. 2:15). "Let us walk honestly, as in the day; not in rioting and drunkenness" (Rom. 13:13). "Nor drunkards shall inherit the kingdom of God" (1 Cor. 6:10).

2. Drunkenness destroys the **body**. "Your body is the temple of the Holy Spirit" (1 cor. 6:19). Whatever harms God's temple is wrong.

3. Drunkenness destroys **morals and integrity** of people. Statistical link between drunkenness and crime, i.e., not those who are guilty of drunkenness will commit crime, but those who commit crimes will probably drink excessively.

4. Drunkenness destroys **self-control** of people.

   a. "The fruit of the Spirit is...self-control" (Gal. 5:23). The word *temperance* that characterized the anti-drunkenness movement means "self-control."

   b. "Be temperate (self-controlled) in all things" (1 Cor. 9:25).

   c. The Bible does not use the term alcoholics (medical term), but drunkards (moral term).

5. Drunkenness is contrary to the **example of Christ**. "Christ...an example, that we should follow His steps" (1 Peter 2:21).

6. Alcohol is **addictive**.

   a. Alcohol is an anesthetic to kill pain and tranquilize.

   b. Alcohol makes a person dependent. One in eight heavy drinkers becomes an alcoholic (1) Psychological compulsive, (2) Sociological compulsive, and (3) Physical compulsive.

C. TWO KINDS OF WINE

Should a Christian drink non-alcoholic beer?

1. **Strong** wine – "violence" (Prov. 23:29-30); "venomous poison" (Prov. 23:31); "sick with wine" (Hosea 7:5); "cup of fury" (Jer. 25:15).

2. **Good** wine – "best" (Num. 18;12), "sweet savor" (Neh. 10:37); "new wine" (Neh. 10:39); "wine of prosperity" (Gen. 27:28; Deut. 11:14); "cheers" (Judges 9:13); "makes glad" (Ps. 104:14-15). The purpose of good wine:

   a. Offering to God (Num. 18;12).

   b. Quenches the thirst (Gen. 27:28).

   c. Symbol of prosperity and the Holy Spirit (Prov. 34:15; Judges 9:13; Prov. 9:2; Eph. 5:17).

3. The difference was **fermentation**. "Fermentation is the result of the natural interaction of yeast (leaven) with the sugars and acid of the juice. As the liquid ferments in the presence of the grape skins...each passing hour in flavor, in color, in aroma, and in body which the winemaker monitors constantly. Fermentation causes heat (70 degrees), and the skins form a cap to produce body. When the right taste is reached, the temperature is reduced to stop fermentation." ~Ernest and Julio Gallo.

4. Leaven **prohibited** (usually rotting skins, i.e., yeast).

   a. Leaven was a sign of <u>sin</u> (Matt. 13:33).

   b. Leaven was prohibited for six days before the **Passover** (Ex. 12:8; 15-20; 13:6-7).

D. DID JESUS CONDONE WINE DRINKING?

1. Jesus served intoxicating wine at the Last Supper . If Jesus served wine that was slightly intoxicating, it opens the door for beer or social drinking today.

   a. **Preparation** argument – leaven strictly prohibited during Passover week.

   b. **Command** argument – "Woe to him who gives drink to his neighbor" (Hab. 2:15).

   c. **Implicit** argument – it is never called wine but the cup or fruit of the vine.

2. Jesus created intoxicating wine at the wedding in Canna because they kept "the good wine until now" (John 2:11).

   a. **Social** argument – family affair would prohibit strong drink.

   b. **Process** argument – juice comes from the clouds into the earth up through the vine, but Christ speeded the process instantaneously. Fermentation is a human additive; Christ used the process of nature.

   c. **Command** argument – "Do not look on the wine when it is red, when it swirls around smoothly" (Prov. 23:31).

3. The enemies claim, "The Son of Man came eating and drinking, and they say, 'Look, a glutton and a winebibber'" (Matt. 11:19).

   a. This is from His **enemies**. "Then the Jews answered and said to Him, 'Do we not say rightly that You are a Samaritan and have a demon?'" (John 8:48).

   b. This is a **comparison** with John the Baptist who was a Nazarite, i.e., no sweet wine.

E. HOW TO BE SOBER LIFE-LONG

What would you tell a new Christian about alcohol?

1. **Know** – right thinking produces right action, i.e., realize that strong drink is prohibited in Scriptures.

2. Be **fearful**. No one knows if they are addicted.

3. Follow the **example** of Christ.

4. Make a **commitment** to your future/present spouse of an "alcohol free" home.

5. **Promise** yourself you will never take your first or another drink of alcohol.

6. Be **careful** of alcohol influenced attractions, i.e., cooking with it, alcohol-free beer, etc.

7. **Bend over backwards** when in an alcohol environment, "Avoid the appearance of evil (1 Thess. 5:22).

Lesson 4:

ALCOHOL: CAN WE DRINK?

A. INTRODUCTION

Should alcoholic products like tobacco products be banned from television advertisements?

1. _____ is the greatest drug problem, not crack, meth, marijuana, etc.

2. _____ . It is impossible for the young man to start right. "In the days of Noah, they were...eating and drinking" (Matt. 24:37-38). But later in life after the flood, "He (Noah) drank of the wine and was drunken" (Gen. 9:21).

3. When a pregnant woman gets drunk, so does her baby. Fifty-two percent of all alcoholics had
_____ .

B. WHY I AM AGAINST LIQUOR

What are the primary reasons for not drinking alcohol products?

1. God _____ drunkenness. Be not drunk with wine wherein is excess but be filled with the Sprit" (Eph. 5:18). "Do not look on the wine when it is red, when it sparkles in the cup" (Prov. 23:31). "Their wine is the poison" (Deut. 32:33). "Woe to him who gives drink to his neighbor, pressing him to your bottle" (Hab. 2:15). "Let us walk honestly, as in the day; not in rioting and drunkenness" (Rom. 13:13). "Nor drunkards shall inherit the kingdom of God" (1 Cor. 6:10).

2. Drunkenness destroys the _____ . "Your body is the temple of the Holy Spirit" (1 Cor. 6:19). Whatever harms God's temple is wrong.

3. Drunkenness destroys _____ of people. Statistical link between drunkenness and crime, i.e., not those who are guilty of drunkenness will commit crime, but those who commit crimes will probably drink excessively.

4. Drunkenness destroys _____ of people.

   a. "The fruit of the Spirit is...self-control" (Gal. 5:23). The word *temperance* that characterized the anti-drunkenness movement means "self-control."

   b. "Be temperate (self-controlled) in all things" (1 Cor. 9:25).

   c. The Bible does not use the term alcoholics (medical term), but drunkards (moral term).

5. Drunkenness is contrary to the _____ . "Christ...an example, that we should follow His steps" (1 Peter 2:21).

6. Alcohol is _____ .

   a. Alcohol is an anesthetic to kill pain and tranquilize.

   b. Alcohol makes a person dependent. One in eight heavy drinkers becomes an alcoholic (1) Psychological compulsive, (2) Sociological compulsive, and (3) Physical compulsive.

C. TWO KINDS OF WINE

Should a Christian drink non-alcoholic beer?

1. _____ wine – "violence" (Prov. 23:29-30); "venomous poison" (Prov. 23:31); "sick with wine" (Hosea 7:5); "cup of fury" (Jer. 25:15).

2. _____ wine – "best" (Num. 18;12), "sweet savor" (Neh. 10:37); "new wine" (Neh. 10:39); "wine of prosperity" (Gen. 27:28; Deut. 11:14); "cheers" (Judges 9:13); "makes glad" (Ps. 104:14-15). The purpose of good wine:

   a. Offering to God (Num. 18;12).

   b. Quenches the thirst (Gen. 27:28).

   c. Symbol of prosperity and the Holy Spirit (Prov. 34:15; Judges 9:13; Prov. 9:2; Eph. 5:17).

3. The difference was _____ . "Fermentation is the result of the natural interaction of yeast (leaven) with the sugars and acid of the juice. As the liquid ferments in the presence of the grape skins... each passing hour in flavor, in color, in aroma, and in body which the winemaker monitors constantly. Fermentation causes heat (70 degrees), and the skins form a cap to produce body. When the right taste is reached, the temperature is reduced to stop fermentation." —Ernest and Julio Gallo.

4. Leaven _____ (usually rotting skins, i.e., yeast).

    a. Leaven was a sign of _____ (Matt. 13:33).

    b. Leaven was prohibited for six days before the _____ (Ex. 12:8; 15-20; 13:6-7).

D. DID JESUS CONDONE WINE DRINKING?

1. Jesus served intoxicating wine at the Last Supper . If Jesus served wine that was slightly intoxicating, it opens the door for beer or social drinking today.

    a. _____ argument – leaven strictly prohibited during Passover week.

    b. _____ argument – "Woe to him who gives drink to his neighbor" (Hab. 2:15).

    c. _____ argument – it is never called wine but the cup or fruit of the vine.

2. Jesus created intoxicating wine at the wedding in Canna because they kept "the good wine until now" (John 2:11).

    a. _____ argument – family affair would prohibit strong drink.

    b. _____ argument – juice comes from the clouds into the earth up through the vine, but Christ speeded the process instantaneously. Fermentation is a human additive; Christ used the process of nature.

    c. _____ argument – "Do not look on the wine when it is red, when it swirls around smoothly" (Prov. 23:31).

3. The enemies claim, "The Son of Man came eating and drinking, and they say, 'Look, a glutton and a winebibber'" (Matt. 11:19).

    a. This is from His _____ . "Then the Jews answered and said to Him, 'Do we not say rightly that You are a Samaritan and have a demon?'" (John 8:48).

    b. This is a _____ with John the Baptist who was a Nazarite, i.e., no sweet wine.

E. HOW TO BE SOBER LIFE-LONG

What would you tell a new Christian about alcohol?

1. _____ – right thinking produces right action, i.e., realize that strong drink is prohibited in Scriptures.

2. Be _____ . No one knows if they are addicted.

3. Follow the _____ of Christ.

4. Make a _____ to your future/present spouse of an "alcohol free" home.

5. _____ yourself you will never take your first or another drink of alcohol.

6. Be _____ of alcohol influenced attractions, i.e., cooking with it, alcohol-free beer, etc.

7. _____ when in an alcohol environment, "Avoid the appearance of evil (1 Thess. 5:22).

Lesson 5:

LANGUAGE

A. INTRODUCTION

As America becomes more secular, she also becomes more hostile to Christianity. No negative influences are more evident of this attack than the filthy speech movement, including profanity and blasphemy.

B. DEFINITION

1. <u>Swearing</u> – to utter and oath or declaration with an appeal to God or a sacred object; to direct judgment for mere emphasis.

2. <u>Cursing</u> – to ask God to bring harm or evil to a person or object; to speak blasphemy. A curse carries its own power of execution. The opposite of "to bless."

3. <u>Blasphemy</u> – to direct curses or judgment toward God or His sacred object.

4. <u>Filthy language</u> – morally vile or obscene language toward parts of the body to convey the idea of disgust.

5. <u>Profanity</u> – bridges the gap between swearing and filthy language. To show utter disregard for God.

6. <u>Slang</u> – language markedly colloquial, regarding the standards of cultural speech, having meaning to those within the "in group."

C. OBSERVATIONS FROM LIFE

1. Swearing no longer dominates only **boys**.

2. One out of 14 college students' words are **swear words**.

3. **Upper** class groups are least likely to swear.

4. Research – children tend to swear from **hearing their parents** swear.

5. American civil Liberties Union (ACLU) has successfully challenged laws dealing with profanity.

D. BIBLICAL OBSERVATIONS

1. "You shall not take the name of the Lord your God in vain, for the Lord will not hold him **guiltless** who takes His name in vain" (Ex. 20:7).

   a. **Vain** – to waste, disorder, empty, or to use God's name for lying or false swearing.

   b. **Guiltless** – allow to go unpunished.

2. **Blasphemy** – punishable by stoning (Lev. 24:10-16).

3. "Michael the archangel, in contending with the devil, when he disputed about the body of Moses, dared not bring against him a **reviling accusation**, but said, 'The Lord rebuke you!'" (Jude 9).

4. Peter – " Then he began to call down curses, and he swore to them" (Matt. 26:74, NIV).

5. Jesus – "Bless them which curse you" (Luke 6:24).

6. Paul – "Neither filthiness nor foolish talking" (Eph. 5:4).

7. "But now you yourselves are to put off all these: anger, wrath, malice, blasphemy, filthy language out of your mouth" (Col. 3:8).

E. WHY PEOPLE USE WRONG LANGUAGE

1. Stirring up **authorities** quoted in *Time Magazine*. It is motivated by:

    a. **Rebellion** against restraints.

    b. Desire for **freedom** or independence.

2. Expression of **anger**. The deeper the rage, the more vicious the language.

3. **Equalize** – a tool of feminism to demonstrate equalization between men and women, quoted in *Time Magazine*.

4. Flaunt **superiority** – it is considered a statement.

5. **Habit** – it represents sub-verbal urges or is the result of modeling by an adult role mode.

6. **Rebellion** against God. "But those things which proceed out of the mouth come from the heart, and they defile a man. For out of the heart proceed evil thoughts, murders, adulteries, fornications, thefts, false witness, blasphemies" (Matt. 15:18-19).

F. TWELVE STEPS TO PROPER SPEECH

1. A believer must **realize** his or her language is wrong. Until there is motivation against a bad habit, there is no motivation toward a good habit.

2. Even though some words have evolved into acceptance by society, the Christian **should not lead** in their use.

3. Try to be **proper** in all things. Learn and use words properly according to God's Word and culture.

4. Avoid striving for **acceptance** among the unchurched by suing their words, symbols, and speech patterns.

5. Realize wrong language will **interfere** with your growth in Christ and testimony to the world.

6. Remember all your speech **reflects** your inner person.

7. Pick out a Christian **role model** to follow in all things. Paul said, "Be followers of me, even as I also am of Christ" (1 Cor. 11:1). "The things which you learned and received and heard (Paul had good language) and saw in me, these do" (Phil. 4:9).

8. Stop watching **bad** movies and television shows.

9. Get **smart**. "Bad language is a dead giver away that the user is showing their ignorance" —*Saturday Review*.

10. Don't separate from cursers but **avoid** their language and be a wholesome testimony. "Let no corrupt word proceed out of your mouth, but what is good for necessary [a]edification, that it may impart grace to the hearers" (Eph. 4:29).

11. Be **careful**. "Let your speech be always with grace, seasoned with salt, that you may know how to answer every man" (Col. 4:6).

12. Memorize and **mediate** on Scriptures. "Let the word of Christ dwell in you richly in all wisdom, teaching and admonishing one another in psalms and hymns and spiritual songs, singing with grace in your hearts to the Lord. And whatever you do in word or deed, do all in the name of the Lord Jesus, giving thanks to God the Father through Him" (Col. 3:16-17).

Lesson 5:

LANGUAGE

A. INTRODUCTION

As America becomes more secular, she also becomes more hostile to Christianity. No negative influences are more evident of this attack than the filthy speech movement, including profanity and blasphemy.

B. DEFINITION

1. _____ – to utter and oath or declaration with an appeal to God or a sacred object; to direct judgment for mere emphasis.

2. _____ – to ask God to bring harm or evil to a person or object; to speak blasphemy. A curse carries its own power of execution. The opposite of "to bless."

3. _____ – to direct curses or judgment toward God or His sacred object.

4. _____ – morally vile or obscene language toward parts of the body to convey the idea of disgust.

5. _____ – bridges the gap between swearing and filthy language. To show utter disregard for God.

6. _____ – language markedly colloquial, regarding the standards of cultural speech, having meaning to those within the "in group."

C. OBSERVATIONS FROM LIFE

1. Swearing no longer dominates only _____ .

2. One out of 14 college students' words are _____ .

3. _____ class groups are least likely to swear.

4. Research – children tend to swear from _____ swear.

5. American civil Liberties Union (ACLU) has successfully challenged laws dealing with profanity.

D. BIBLICAL OBSERVATIONS

1. "You shall not take the name of the Lord your God in vain, for the Lord will not hold him _____ who takes His name in vain" (Ex. 20:7).

   a. _____ – to waste, disorder, empty, or to use God's name for lying or false swearing.

   b. _____ – allow to go unpunished.

2. _____ – punishable by stoning (Lev. 24:10-16).

3. "Michael the archangel, in contending with the devil, when he disputed about the body of Moses, dared not bring against him a _____ , but said, 'The Lord rebuke you!'" (Jude 9).

4. Peter – " Then he began to call down curses, and he swore to them" (Matt. 26:74, NIV).

5. Jesus – "Bless them which curse you" (Luke 6:24).

6. Paul – "Neither filthiness nor foolish talking" (Eph. 5:4).

7. "But now you yourselves are to put off all these: anger, wrath, malice, blasphemy, filthy language out of your mouth" (Col. 3:8).

E. WHY PEOPLE USE WRONG LANGUAGE

1. Stirring up _____ quoted in *Time Magazine*. It is motivated by:

   a. _____ against restraints.

   b. Desire for _____ or independence.

2. Expression of _____ . The deeper the rage, the more vicious the language.

3. _____ – a tool of feminism to demonstrate equalization between men and women, quoted in *Time Magazine*.

4. Flaunt _____ – it is considered a statement.

5. _____ – it represents sub-verbal urges or is the result of modeling by an adult role mode.

6. _____ against God. "But those things which proceed out of the mouth come from the heart, and they defile a man. For out of the heart proceed evil thoughts, murders, adulteries, fornications, thefts, false witness, blasphemies" (Matt. 15:18-19).

F. TWELVE STEPS TO PROPER SPEECH

1. A believer must _____ his or her language is wrong. Until there is motivation against a bad habit, there is no motivation toward a good habit.

2. Even though some words have evolved into acceptance by society, the Christian _____ in their use.

3. Try to be _____ in all things. Learn and use words properly according to God's Word and culture.

4. Avoid striving for _____ among the unchurched by suing their words, symbols, and speech patterns.

5. Realize wrong language will _____ with your growth in Christ and testimony to the world.

6. Remember all your speech _____ your inner person.

7. Pick out a Christian _____ to follow in all things. Paul said, "Be followers of me, even as I also am of Christ" (1 Cor. 11:1). "The things which you learned and received and heard (Paul had good language) and saw in me, these do" (Phil. 4:9).

8. Stop watching _____ movies and television shows.

9. Get _____ . "Bad language is a dead giver away that the user is showing their ignorance" —*Saturday Review*.

10. Don't separate from cursers but **<u>avoid</u>** their language and be a wholesome testimony. "Let no corrupt word proceed out of your mouth, but what is good for necessary [a]edification, that it may impart grace to the hearers" (Eph. 4:29).

11. Be _____ . "Let your speech be always with grace, seasoned with salt, that you may know how to answer every man" (Col. 4:6).

12. Memorize and _____ on Scriptures. "Let the word of Christ dwell in you richly in all wisdom, teaching and admonishing one another in psalms and hymns and spiritual songs, singing with grace in your hearts to the Lord. And whatever you do in word or deed, do all in the name of the Lord Jesus, giving thanks to God the Father through Him" (Col. 3:16-17).

DANCING

A. INTRODUCTION

1. Definition: "A series of rhythmic and patterned bodily movements performed to music." ~Webster

2. Biblical dances – An emotional and physical expression of the entire body in rhythmic movement to music for a specific purpose. "Then David danced before the Lord" (2 Sam. 6:14).

   a. What is your purpose? **David danced to God**.

   b. What are you expressing? **Praise and gratitude**.

   c. How are you moving? **Positive feelings before God**.

3. In the 50s **hugging**; in the 70s **separate**; in the 90s (Madonna and Michael Jackson) **alone**.

B. UNACCEPTABLE DANCING IN THE BIBLE

1. **Rebellion**. "He saw the calf and the dancing. So, Moses' anger became hot, and he cast the tablets out of his hands and broke them at the foot of the mountain" (Ex. 32:19).

2. **Seduction**. "When Herodias' daughter...came in and danced, and pleased Herod and those who sat with him" (Mark 6:22).

C. ACCEPTABLE DANCING IN THE BIBLE

1. Expression of __praise__. "Let them praise His name in the dance" (Ps. 149:3, 150:4).

2. Sometimes __acceptable__. "A time to weep, a time to laugh; a time to mourn, a time to dance" (Ecc. 3:4). Dancing associated with joyful emotions.

3. Acceptable __description__. "We have piped unto you and ye have not danced"(Matt. 11:17).

4. Symbol of __happiness__. "Thou hast turned for me my mourning into dancing" (Ps. 20:11).

D. TEST FOR DANCING

1. The following tests should be applied to situations that involve dancing. The __thought__ test. The greatest appeal of Christianity is to the mind or the appeal of truth. We are thinking people made in the image of a rational God. What you think is imperative. Ask, "what are you thinking when you participate in this dance?" "Whatsoever things are true...honest...just ...pure...lovely...good report, if there be any virtue, if there be any praise, think on these things" (Phil. 14:8).

2. The __message__ test. All music makes a statement. Ask, "what is being said by the words and music?"

3. The __desire__ test. Ask yourself, "what does this dance do to my desires? Two more questions flow out of the first. "Does this dance arouse my lust toward my partner or someone else?" Second, "does this dancing lower my resistance so that I may participate in other lustful dancing or other harmful activities?" "But each one is tempted when he is drawn away by his own desires and enticed. Then, when desire has conceived, it gives birth to sin; and sin, when it is full-grown, brings forth death" (James 1:14-15).

4. The __association__ test. Ask yourself, "should I be around the people I am dancing with?" "Should I be dancing with this person?" "Should I be associated with the music's artist?"

5. The __place__ test. You have to ask, "Should I be in the place where I am dancing?" This may or may not be a physical place, but a circumstance. "Do you not know that friendship with the world is enmity with God?" (James 4:4). While a place is not evil, what is evil is the believer's support of evil in that place and the believer's identification with evil in a place. Jesus explained, "I do not pray that You should take them out of the world, but that You should keep them from the evil one" (John 17:15).

6. The __testimony__ test Ask, "What will my dancing do to other people?" Your freedom may harm another. "But beware lest somehow this liberty of yours become a stumbling block to those who are weak" (1 Cor. 8:9).

7. The **music** test. All music has "the song within the song." Is this good music or poor music?

Lesson 6:

DANCING

A. INTRODUCTION

1. Definition: "A series of rhythmic and patterned bodily movements performed to music." —Webster

2. Biblical dances – An emotional and physical expression of the entire body in rhythmic movement to music for a specific purpose. "Then David danced before the Lord" (2 Sam. 6:14).

   a. What is your purpose? _____ .

   b. What are you expressing? _____ .

   c. How are you moving? _____ .

3. In the 50s _____ ; in the 70s _____ ; in the 90s (Madonna and Michael Jackson) _____ .

B. UNACCEPTABLE DANCING IN THE BIBLE

1. _____ . "He saw the calf and the dancing. So, Moses' anger became hot, and he cast the tablets out of his hands and broke them at the foot of the mountain" (Ex. 32:19).

2. _____ . "When Herodias' daughter...came in and danced, and pleased Herod and those who sat with him" (Mark 6:22).

C. ACCEPTABLE DANCING IN THE BIBLE

1. Expression of _____ . "Let them praise His name in the dance" (Ps. 149:3, 150:4).

2. Sometimes _____ . "A time to weep, a time to laugh; a time to mourn, a time to dance" (Ecc. 3:4). Dancing associated with joyful emotions.

3. Acceptable _____ . "We have piped unto you and ye have not danced"(Matt. 11:17).

4. Symbol of _____ . "Thou hast turned for me my mourning into dancing" (Ps. 20:11).

D. TEST FOR DANCING

1. The following tests should be applied to situations that involve dancing. The _____ test. The greatest appeal of Christianity is to the mind or the appeal of truth. We are thinking people made in the image of a rational God. What you think is imperative. Ask, "what are you thinking when you participate in this dance?" "Whatsoever things are true...honest...just ...pure...lovely...good report, if there be any virtue, if there be any praise, think on these things" (Phil. 14:8).

2. The _____ test. All music makes a statement. Ask, "what is being said by the words and music?"

3. The _____ test. Ask yourself, "what does this dance do to my desires? Two more questions flow out of the first. "Does this dance arouse my lust toward my partner or someone else?" Second, "does this dancing lower my resistance so that I may participate in other lustful dancing or other harmful activities?" "But each one is tempted when he is drawn away by his own desires and enticed. Then, when desire has conceived, it gives birth to sin; and sin, when it is full-grown, brings forth death" (James 1:14-15).

4. The _____ test. Ask yourself, "should I be around the people I am dancing with?" "Should I be dancing with this person?" "Should I be associated with the music's artist?"

5. The _____ test. You have to ask, "Should I be in the place where I am dancing?" This may or may not be a physical place, but a circumstance. "Do you not know that friendship with the world is enmity with God?" (James 4:4). While a place is not evil, what is evil is the believer's support of evil in that place and the believer's identification with evil in a place. Jesus explained, "I do not pray that You should take them out of the world, but that You should keep them from the evil one" (John 17:15).

6. The _____ test Ask, "What will my dancing do to other people?" Your freedom may harm another. "But beware lest somehow this liberty of yours become a stumbling block to those who are weak" (1 Cor. 8:9).

7. The _____ test. All music has "the song within the song." Is this good music or poor music?

LIES

A. INTRODUCTION

1. **Root and fruit**. No one teaches small children to lie. You lie because you have a lying nature, not because you became a liar, but because you told an untruth. All men are liars (Ps. 116:11).

2. Those who lie make it twice on God's list. "Six things the Lord hates, yes, seven are an abomination to Him…(1) a lying tongue…(2) a false witness who speaks lies" (Prov. 6:16-19).

B. THREE DEFINITIONS OF LYING

1. **Active**. "To make an untrue statement with the intent to deceive." ~Webster

2. **Passive**. To create a false, or misleading impression.

3. **Inner**. To tolerate internal compromise with what you know is right.

C. FOUR STEPS OF A LIE

1. To **create** deceit. You begin to calculate or make-up a life.

2. To relay **dishonesty**. You communicate to another something that is not truth, i.e., a lie.

3. **Intend** to mislead or misrepresent.

4. Avoid moral **responsibly**. A lie is conspiracy participating in a cover up or falsehood. But those who do so, know what they do and are responsible to themselves and to God.

D. JUDGING THE TYPES OF LIES

1. <u>White</u> lies. Telling an untruth to deceive, but for a good purpose.

2. <u>Political</u> lies. Telling an untruth to flatter or not telling the truth to keep from embarrassing someone.

3. <u>Gossip</u> lies. To tell what should not be told with a selfish purpose.

4. <u>Sinister</u> lies. To seek to hear things that are not true and pass them on to harm another.

5. <u>Jovial</u> lies. An obvious untruth to all for the purpose of humor and enjoyment.

6. <u>Half</u> lies. To not tell al with the intent to deceive.

7. <u>Excuses</u> lies. To give reason or explanation that may or may not be the primary cause.

8. <u>Hypocrisy</u> lies to claim to be something that is contrary to your life.

9. <u>Justifying</u> lies. If I lie about my numbers, and you know that I lied, and I know you know that I lied, isn't that like telling the truth.

10. <u>Face-saving</u> lies. "Sarah laughed within herself" (Gen. 1:12). "The Lord said, 'wherefore did Sarah laugh?'" (v. 13). "Sarah denied...'I laughed not'" (v. 15).

11. <u>Evangelistic</u> lies. "Peter said to Ananias, 'Ananias, why has Satan filled your heart to lie to the Holy Spirit?'" (Acts 5:3). Theoretically, you cannot lie to God because He knows everything.

12. <u>Propaganda</u> lies. You give your side of the truth but ignore or hide the other side.

13. <u>Advertisement</u> lies. Persuading people of the benefits not considering the limitations or qualifications.

14. <u>Cheating</u> lies. To claim something that does not belong to you.

15. <u>Demonic</u> lies. When you call truth a lie, and you present a lie as truth. "Send them strong delusion, that they should believe the lie" (2 Thess. 2:11). "Who exchanged the truth of God for the lie" (Rom. 1:25).

16. Put a <u>spin</u> on the truth. You tell a negative story in a way that makes you look good.

ˉE. HOW TO OVERCOME THE HABIT OF LYING

1. Look to the **standard**. "I am the...truth" (Jesus).

2. Realize the **source** of lying. You are of your father the devil...he is a liar" (John 8:44).

3. Admit your **nature** is deceitful. "The heart is deceitful and desperately wicked" (Jer. 17:9). "For out of the heart proceeds evil thoughts...false witness" (Matt. 15:19).

4. Recognize the **fate** of liars. "But the fearful and unbelievers...and all liars shall have their part in the lake which burns with fire" (Rev. 21:8).

5. Respond to your **obligation**. "Therefore, putting away lying, 'Let each one of you speak truth with his neighbor,' for we are members of one another" (Eph. 4:25).

6. Determine to be a **radical** disciple. "If anyone desires to come after Me, let him deny himself, and take up his cross daily, and follow Me" (Luke 9:23).

7. Walk in **forgiveness**. God knows "all men are liars" but in mercy forgives all. "They (Israel) lied to Him (God) with their tongues...but He, being full of compassion, forgave their iniquity" (Ps. 78:36-38).

8. Ask for **strength**. "Our Father...forgive us our debts" (Matt. 6:9-12).

9. Make a **decision** to tell the truth. There is power in a simple decision made by the total person.

10. Resolve to be a person of **character**. The worst thing I life is to allow internal compromise.

    a. Others cannot trust you if you don't trust yourself.

    b. If your self-wroth deteriorates, you cannot direct yourself.

LIES

A. INTRODUCTION

1. _____ . No one teaches small children to lie. You lie because you have a lying nature, not because you became a liar, but because you told an untruth. All men are liars (Ps. 116:11).

2. Those who lie make it twice on God's list. "Six things the Lord hates, yes, seven are an abomination to Him...(1) a lying tongue...(2) a false witness who speaks lies" (Prov. 6:16-19).

B. THREE DEFINITIONS OF LYING

1. _____ . "To make an untrue statement with the intent to deceive." —Webster

2. _____ . To create a false, or misleading impression.

3. _____ . To tolerate internal compromise with what you know is right.

C. FOUR STEPS OF A LIE

1. To _____ deceit. You begin to calculate or make-up a life.

2. To relay _____ . You communicate to another something that is not truth, i.e., a lie.

3. _____ to mislead or misrepresent.

4. Avoid moral _____ . A lie is conspiracy participating in a cover up or falsehood. But those who do so, know what they do and are responsible to themselves and to God.

D. JUDGING THE TYPES OF LIES

1. _____ lies. Telling an untruth to deceive, but for a good purpose.

2. _____ lies. Telling an untruth to flatter or not telling the truth to keep from embarrassing someone.

3. _____ lies. To tell what should not be told with a selfish purpose.

4. _____ lies. To seek to hear things that are not true and pass them on to harm another.

5. _____ lies. An obvious untruth to all for the purpose of humor and enjoyment.

6. _____ lies. To not tell al with the intent to deceive.

7. _____ lies. To give reason or explanation that may or may not be the primary cause.

8. _____ lies to claim to be something that is contrary to your life.

9. _____ lies. If I lie about my numbers, and you know that I lied, and I know you know that I lied, isn't that like telling the truth.

10. _____ lies. "Sarah laughed within herself" (Gen. 1:12). "The Lord said, 'wherefore did Sarah laugh?'" (v. 13). "Sarah denied...'I laughed not'" (v. 15).

11. _____ lies. "Peter said to Ananias, 'Ananias, why has Satan filled your heart to lie to the Holy Spirit?'" (Acts 5:3). Theoretically, you cannot lie to God because He knows everything.

12. _____ lies. You give your side of the truth but ignore or hide the other side.

13. _____ lies. Persuading people of the benefits not considering the limitations or qualifications.

14. _____ lies. To claim something that does not belong to you.

15. _____ lies. When you call truth a lie, and you present a lie as truth. "Send them strong delusion, that they should believe the lie" (2 Thess. 2:11). "Who exchanged the truth of God for the lie" (Rom. 1:25).

16. Put a _____ on the truth. You tell a negative story in a way that makes you look good.

E. HOW TO OVERCOME THE HABIT OF LYING

1. Look to the _____ . "I am the...truth" (Jesus).

2. Realize the _____ of lying. You are of your father the devil...he is a liar" (John 8:44).

3. Admit your _____ is deceitful. "The heart is deceitful and desperately wicked" (Jer. 17:9). "For out of the heart proceeds evil thoughts...false witness" (Matt. 15:19).

4. Recognize the _____ of liars. "But the fearful and unbelievers...and all liars shall have their part in the lake which burns with fire" (Rev. 21:8).

5. Respond to your _____ . "Therefore, putting away lying, 'Let each one of you speak truth with his neighbor,' for we are members of one another" (Eph. 4:25).

6. Determine to be a _____ disciple. "If anyone desires to come after Me, let him deny himself, and take up his cross daily, and follow Me" (Luke 9:23).

7. Walk in _____ . God knows "all men are liars" but in mercy forgives all. "They (Israel) lied to Him (God) with their tongues...but He, being full of compassion, forgave their iniquity" (Ps. 78:36-38).

8. Ask for _____ . "Our Father...forgive us our debts" (Matt. 6:9-12).

9. Make a _____ to tell the truth. There is power in a simple decision made by the total person.

10. Resolve to be a person of _____ . The worst thing I life is to allow internal compromise.

    a. Others cannot trust you if you don't trust yourself.

    b. If your self-wroth deteriorates, you cannot direct yourself.

Lesson 8:

RACISM

A. INTRODUCTION

1. Definition:

   a. **Discriminate**. "To make a difference in treatment or favor on a basis rather than merit" —Webster.

   b. **Racism** – "Belief that racial difference produces an inherent superiority of a particular race" —Webster.

   c. Synonyms for race – nations, Gentiles, ethnic groups, people groups, family, class, tribe.

2. First mention. "The Gentiles were divided in their lands, everyone by his tongue, after their families in their nations" (Gen. 10:5). "I will make of thee (Abraham) a great nation" (Gen. 12:2).

3. Biological **source**. Why are there different races?

   a. **Creation**, but God created only two, Adam and Eve. All others come from some source.

   b. **Environment**. The sun made the Africans black and the Scandinavians blond-haired and washed skin. But the original genetics do not return when environment changes.

   c. Embryonic difference were innate in first created person. "Adam is the head of the human race." And environmental differences were reinforced by environment, sovereignly assigned by God.

4. Theological **source**. God made us different. "When the Most High divided the nations (races) their inheritance...He set the bounds of the people according to the number of the children of Israel"(Deut. 32:9). The number of races ahs something to do with Jews.

5. Why different in races?

    a. Every person is made in the image of God. "Let Us make man in Our image after Our likeness" (Gen. 1:26). But no one person **perfectly reflects** God. The great intellectual person reflects God's mind, and the deeply emotional mother reflects God's love. We understand God's love from a broader perspective of various people.

    b. Every race reflects a **different** aspect of God. The self-disciplined oriental, the entrepreneurial driven Anglo, or the hospitable Egyptian. You must see all races to get a broad view of God.

    c. Since God made us all like Himself, it is **anti-faith** to dislike one race, for you deny the purpose and nature of God.

6. Priority of **evangelism**. Jesus commanded to plant churches for all races, "Go therefore and make disciples of all races" (Matt. 28;19). Jesus commanded to evangelize every person, "Go...preach the Gospel to every creature"(Matt. 16:15).

7. Races in **Heaven**. You will keep your racial characteristics in Heaven. "The leaves of the tree were for the healing (growth) of the races" (Rev. 22:2). "They sang a new song...You...have redeemed us to God by Your blood out of every tribe and tongue and people and nation" (Rev. 5:9). "I beheld a great multitude...of all nations (races) and kindred, and people, and tongues"(Rev. 7:9).

B. PROBLEM OF GROWING RACISM/VIOLENCE

Depression Kids	Baby Boomers	Busters
1925-1945	1945-1965	1965-1985
Last segregated	Integrated	Racist
War mentality	Idealistic	Violent
Won WWII	Hated Vietnam	Wins Vietnam
Conservative	Optimistic	Pessimistic

1. The five steps of racism:

    a. **Inward** – you value your race as superior based on racial differences to another.

    b. **Outward** – you devalue another person with less value.

    c. **Expression** – you act, decide, express opinions or make outward actions to them.

    d. **Results** – to the detriment of that race, yourself, and your race.

    e. **Compromises** your relationship with God.

2. Trend: <u>increased</u> racism and violence in spite of Boomer song, "*I liked to teach the world to sing in perfect harmony.*"

3. Why? Race relations prosper when righteous laws are enforced equally to the benefit of all.

    a. Law subdues ancient **hatred**.

    b. Decline in the influence of Christianity.

    c. Blindness to needs of some.

    d. Ineffectiveness or unbalanced media.

    e. **Pride** (ethnocentrism).

    f. Fear.

    g. **Ignorance**.

    h. Ethnic cleansing.

    i. Holocaust.

    j. Politically correct.

C. ANSWERS TO RACISM

1. **Command**. "We should love one another" (1 John 2:11).

2. Example of **Christ**. "How is it that You, being a Jew, ask a drink from me, a Samaritan woman?" (John 4:9).

3. Cross-cultural **evangelism**. Never compromise biblical doctrine or enteral principles but adapt methods to reach people where they are and lift them to where they should be.

4. **Regeneration**. "Can anyone forbid water, that these should not be baptized who have received the Holy Spirit just as we have?" (Acts 10:47).

5. New **position**. "There is neither Greek nor Jew, circumcised nor uncircumcised, barbarian, Scythian, slave nor free, but Christ is all and in all" (Col. 3:11). "There is neither Jew nor Greek...neither male nor female; for you are all one in Christ Jesus." (Gal. 3:28).

6. Give to others but demand nothing for **yourself**.

7. Remember a race **less fortunate** than yours. Instead of always protecting your race, focus on those less fortunate than your race.

8. Ask for **color blind** eyes. Some races have an advantage over your race, just as yours has advantages.

9. We all have the same **human** characteristic.

Lesson 8:

RACISM

A. INTRODUCTION

1. Definition:

   a. _____ . "To make a difference in treatment or favor on a basis rather than merit" —Webster.

   b. _____ – "Belief that racial difference produces an inherent superiority of a particular race" —Webster.

   c. Synonyms for race – nations, Gentiles, ethnic groups, people groups, family, class, tribe.

2. First mention. "The Gentiles were divided in their lands, everyone by his tongue, after their families in their nations" (Gen. 10:5). "I will make of thee (Abraham) a great nation" (Gen. 12:2).

3. Biological _____ . Why are there different races?

   a. _____ , but God created only two, Adam and Eve. All others come from some source.

   b. _____ . The sun made the Africans black and the Scandinavians blond-haired and washed skin. But the original genetics do not return when environment changes.

   c. Embryonic difference were innate in first created person. "Adam is the head of the human race." And environmental differences were reinforced by environment, sovereignly assigned by God.

4. Theological _____ . God made us different. "When the Most High divided the nations (races) their inheritance...He set the bounds of the people according to the number of the children of Israel"(Deut. 32:9). The number of races ahs something to do with Jews.

5. Why different in races?

   a. Every person is made in the image of God. "Let Us make man in Our image after Our likeness" (Gen. 1:26). But no one person _____ God. The great intellectual person reflects God's mind, and the deeply emotional mother reflects God's love. We understand God's love from a broader perspective of various people.

   b. Every race reflects a _____ aspect of God. The self-disciplined oriental, the entrepreneurial driven Anglo, or the hospitable Egyptian. You must see all races to get a broad view of God.

   c. Since God made us all like Himself, it is _____ to dislike one race, for you deny the purpose and nature of God.

6. Priority of _____ . Jesus commanded to plant churches for all races, "Go therefore and make disciples of all races" (Matt. 28;19). Jesus commanded to evangelize every person, "Go...preach the Gospel to every creature"(Matt. 16:15).

7. Races in _____ . You will keep your racial characteristics in Heaven. "The leaves of the tree were for the healing (growth) of the races" (Rev. 22:2). "They sang a new song...You...have redeemed us to God by Your blood out of every tribe and tongue and people and nation" (Rev. 5:9). "I beheld a great multitude...of all nations (races) and kindred, and people, and tongues"(Rev. 7:9).

B. PROBLEM OF GROWING RACISM/VIOLENCE

Depression Kids	Baby Boomers	Busters
1925-1945	1945-1965	1965-1985
Last segregated	Integrated	Racist
War mentality	Idealistic	Violent
Won WWII	Hated Vietnam	Wins Vietnam
Conservative	Optimistic	Pessimistic

1. The five steps of racism:

   a. _____ – you value your race as superior based on racial differences to another.

   b. _____ – you devalue another person with less value.

   c. _____ – you act, decide, express opinions or make outward actions to them.

   d. _____ – to the detriment of that race, yourself, and your race.

   e. _____ your relationship with God.

2. Trend: _____ racism and violence in spite of Boomer song, "*I liked to teach the world to sing in perfect harmony.*"

3. Why? Race relations prosper when righteous laws are enforced equally to the benefit of all.

   a. Law subdues ancient _____ .

   b. Decline in the influence of Christianity.

   c. Blindness to needs of some.

   d. Ineffectiveness or unbalanced media.

   e. _____ (ethnocentrism).

   f. Fear.

   g. _____ .

   h. Ethnic cleansing.

   i. Holocaust.

   j. Politically correct.

C. ANSWERS TO RACISM

1. _____ . "We should love one another" (1 John 2:11).

2. Example of _____ . "How is it that You, being a Jew, ask a drink from me, a Samaritan woman?" (John 4:9).

3. Cross-cultural _____ . Never compromise biblical doctrine or enteral principles but adapt methods to reach people where they are and lift them to where they should be.

4. _____ . "Can anyone forbid water, that these should not be baptized who have received the Holy Spirit just as we have?" (Acts 10:47).

5. New _____ . "There is neither Greek nor Jew, circumcised nor uncircumcised, barbarian, Scythian, slave nor free, but Christ is all and in all" (Col. 3:11). "There is neither Jew nor Greek... neither male nor female; for you are all one in Christ Jesus." (Gal. 3:28).

6. Give to others but demand nothing for _____ .

7. Remember a race _____ than yours. Instead of always protecting your race, focus on those less fortunate than your race.

8. Ask for _____ eyes. Some races have an advantage over your race, just as yours has advantages.

9. We all have the same _____ characteristic.

PART THREE

WHAT IS RIGHT?

POWERPOINT GUIDE

What is Right?

Biblical Principles for Decision-Making

Slide 1 of 96

Presuppositions and Principles

Slide 2 of 96

A. Introduction

1. This series will deal with issues such as swearing, television, movies, music, dancing, pornography, alcohol, and stretching the truth.

2. Definition: Presupposition is a "self-evident truth" or the acceptance of a "cause" because it is proved by its effect. Synonym: premise, postulate, or basis. Principle is truth in application to life. Synonym: rule or standard.

Slide 3 of 96

B. Biblical Presupposition

1. The source of right: God. Since God is perfect, He cannot be wrong, nor can He direct anyone to a wrong attitude or action. Since God is all-powerful, all-knowing, all-everywhere present, He will direct everyone right.

Slide 4 of 96

---

2. The opposite of right: sin. If there is right, what is its opposite or its violation? Sin is an unpopular word. Our dictionary defines sin only with moral conditions and in relationship with God.
   a. Biblical view of sin is:
      Active and passive
      Commission and omission
      Know and ignorant
   b. Social view: failure, disaster, accident, or survival of the fittest.

Slide 5 of 96

---

3. The motive of right: love. "God is love" 1 John 4:8. Love is described as a positive and beneficial relationship by God for His people.
   a. He cannot make principles to harm us.
   b. He cannot cause principles to mislead us.
   c. He never will introduce principles to withhold good from us.
   d. He may allow circumstances to mature us.

Slide 6 of 96

---

4. The purpose of right: to glorify God. "The chief end of man is to glorify God and enjoy Him forever." Answer to first question. ~*Westminster Catechism*

5. The priority of right: people. God did not give principles just for Himself or nature, but for people. "What is man that You are mindful of him, for You have made him a little lower than the angels, and You have crowned him with glory and honor. You have made him to have dominion over the works of Your hands; You have put all *things* under his feet" (Ps. 8:4-6, *NKJV*).

Slide 7 of 96

---

6. The assurance of right: knowing. Christianity is a rational faith. "Come now let us reason together says the Lord" (Isa. 1:18, *NKJV*). We are made int eh image of God and got our mind from Him.
   a. His principles are "self-evident."
   b. We can know things to the degree we directly observe them.
   c. All mankind is given the same power of thinking, observing, and knowing.
   d. We accept that which is logical and reject that which is illogical.
   e. The world operates as a set of principles, i.e., physics (laws of nature), psychology, sociology, anthropology, logic, etc.

Slide 8 of 96

C. **Biblical Principles**

1. The principle of <u>obeying light</u>. Don't violate a clear scriptural command. "Thou shalt not take the name of the Lord thy God in vain" (Ex. 20:7).

2. The principle of <u>following rules</u>. Don't violate a clear scriptural principle. "Know ye not that your body is the temple of the Holy Spirit" (1 Cor. 6:19).

3. The principle of <u>clean thoughts</u>. Don't allow impure thoughts or deeds. "Whosoever looketh upon a woman to lust after her hath committed adultery with her already in his heart" (Matt. 5:28).

4. The principle of <u>respecting another person</u>. Don't harm another person. "Take heed lest by any means this liberty of yours becomes a stumbling block to them that are weak" (1 Cor. 8:9).

5. The principle of following <u>Christ's example</u>. Follow Christ's example. "Christ . . . leaving us an example, that ye should follow His steps" (1 Peter 2:21).

6. The principle of following your <u>conscience</u>. Don't violate your personal conscience. "God's laws are written within them; their own conscience accuses them; or sometimes excuses them" (Rom. 2:15, *LB*).

7. The principle of <u>internal integrity</u>. Don't harm your inner man. "Anyone who believes that something he wants to do is wrong shouldn't do it, he sins if he does, for he thinks it is wrong, and so for him it is wrong. Anything that is done apart from what he feels is right is sin" (Rom. 14:23, *LB*).

8. The principle of <u>physical integrity</u>. Don't harm your body. "Flee sexual sin. No other sin affects the body as this one does. When you sin this sin, it is against your own body" (1 Cor. 6:19, *LB*).

Lesson 2

Videos, Movies and Television

A. **Introduction**

1. The average American watches television four to five hours a day, seven days a week per home.

2. Transition from three channels to over 900 channels.

3. From reflection of society to change society. From "Father Knows Best" to Madonna and erotic videos.

B. **The Problems of the Media**

1. Learning problems:
   a. <u>Modeling</u>. Children mimic the behavior observed: (1) undermines creativity (Lilian Katz, Ph.D., University of Illinois), (2) assumes destructive orientation to life, and (3) negative becomes greater than positive.
   b. <u>Communication</u> of data. Children see vastly more, yet do not interact with knowledge, understand it or apply it positively.

2. Social problems (research from Lichter, Lichter, and Rothman).
   a. Most businessmen and women are <u>corrupt or dishonest</u>.
   b. Most government <u>officials</u> are obstructive or manipulative.
   c. The sexual adventurer is a cool guy: 1,400 sexual instances each year.
   d. Professionals are sharing, selfness i.e., doctors, layers, journalists.
   e. <u>Minorities</u> are seen as guiltless victims.
   f. "Television is an acid eating away at the base of traditional society" (Lichter, Lichter, and Rothman).

3. Truth, accuracy, and fairness problems. Media does not look at both sides. It is not committed to "the truth, the whole truth, and nothing but the truth."
   a. Television shows 75% of murderers are <u>middle age</u> 90% by <u>whites</u> 60% under 30, and 47% are black (FBI).
   b. <u>Hispanics</u> commit twice as many crimes as any other minorities yet in actuality commit less than 20%.
   c. Television is bias to <u>feminist</u> roles, yet membership in non-feminist organizations is four times higher.
   d. The consequences of <u>violence</u> is not shown, (1) to the victim, (2) to the youthful criminal.

4. Crime problems:
   a. Fifteen years ago, the major crimes of children under 15 was theft, breaking and entering, and property crimes. Now it is drug related crimes.
   b. Television and movies teach disrespect and rebellion to authorities, i.e., police, social workers, judges, etc.
   c. Increase in violence desensitized people (1) to do it, and (2) what it does to people.

d. "I don't take seriously someone begin killed on a show, but it bothers me on the news."
e. Violence in movies targets the 12 to 17-year-old males because they are the chief purchasers of movie tickets.
f. Violent crimes by 12 to 17-year-old males are up 700% since 1962.
g. Because of violence in American cartoons, the Canadian Broadcasting System will not show them.
h. The rise in crime against women is in proportion to its rise in the media.

5. Religious problems:
   a. Ministers are portrayed as (1) ineffective "do-gooders," (2) immoral philanderers, and (3) social miss-fits.
   b. Churches are anti-progressive, legalistic, not enjoyable, and archaic.
   c. Ignored evangelical objections to the last temptation of Christ while media "buckles under" to objection by the NAACP, Jewish lobby, homosexual lobby, and the feminist lobby.
   d. Michael Medved, a Jewish co-host to Sneak Previews on PBS wrote Hollywood vs. America, Harper Collins, and documented movie's immoral and anti-God bias.

C. Solutions:

1. Consumer pressure and boycott. "Hollywood can clean up its act if enough consumers press for reform." ~Michael Medved.

2. Ratings system: God, PG, R, NC-7, X
   a. The choice factor.
   b. The immoral factor.
   c. The harm factor.

3. The education approach.
   a. Support and propagate good ones.
   b. Communicate the harmful effects of bad ones.

4. Censorship (determine what can be shown).
   a. Who will be the censors and who will appoint them?
   b. What will be the standards? 1800s? 1950s? 1980s? Protestant-Puritan ethic? The traditional American ethic?
   c. Christianity in the majority has unflinchingly held to one way of salvation yet is sympathetic and tolerant in ministering to everyone no matter what they believe. Yet when Christianity becomes a minority, it is attacked for intolerance and bias.

5. Separation. "Come out from them and be separate, says the Lord, touch no unclean thing, and I will receive you. I will be a Father to you, and you will be my sons and daughters says the Lord Almighty" (2 Cor. 6:17-18, N IV).
   a. Christianity has no right to assume entertainment will reflect their values, traditions, and faith.
   b. The Christian does not need worldly entertainment; there are other recreations.
   c. The Christian has his or her own art and music, he or she does not need to the world.

6. Stewardship of time, talent, and treasures. Christians have such a great calling; they shouldn't waste their resources on worldly media.

7. Immunization, not isolation. The believer cannot ignore the world (TV), in which he or she lives. In the world, but not of the world. "Not that you would take them out of the world but keep them from evil in the world" (John 17:15, NIV).

D. Warnings:

1. The world will <u>lull</u> us to sleep. Evangelicals are complacent about politics, community life, and entertainment.
2. The world <u>hates</u> us. "If the world hates you, ye know that it hated Me before it hated you."
3. The world will <u>harm</u> us. "Do not love the world or anything in the world. If anyone les the world, the love of the Father is not in him" (1 John 2:15).
4. The world will target our <u>children</u>. Rags to riches in three generations. ~Richard Neibour

Slide 25 of 96

Slide 26 of 96

A. Introduction

Should a Christian listen to and enjoy all songs? When is a song inappropriate for the Christian? While music is amoral, i.e., neither good nor bad, it is usually the context of music that determines its moral nature. This lesson will help the believer determine what kind of music is appropriate for the Christian.

Slide 27 of 96

B. God's Purpose For Music

1. Three types of congregational music:
   a. <u>Scripture</u>.
   b. <u>Worship</u>.
   c. <u>Gospel</u>.

"Teaching and admonishing one another in psalms and hymns and spiritual songs, singing with grace in your hearts to the Lord"
(Col. 3:16).

Slide 28 of 96

2. Private music. "Speaking to one another in psalms and hymns and spiritual songs, singing and making melody in your heart to the Lord" (Eph. 5:19).

3. Who sings Scripture? <u>Youth and high church</u>.
   Who sings worship? <u>Pentecostals and Presbyterians</u>.
   Who sings gospel? <u>Baptist</u>.

Slide 29 of 96

C. What Is Music? (Oxford Dictionary)

1. <u>Melody</u>. "Sounds in agreeable succession." The melody carries the words of the song.
2. <u>Harmony</u> (chords). "A simultaneous combination of tones, chorded structures as distinguished from melody and rhythm." Harmony effects the emotions or mood.
3. <u>Rhythm</u>. "Movement or procedure with uniform recurrence of a beat, accent, or pulse." Rhythm effects the physical. "David would take a harp and play it with his hand. Then Saul would become refreshed" (1 Sam. 16:23).
4. <u>Words</u>. The message that is communicated by the song.

Slide 30 of 96

D. Test To Measure Your Music

1. The <u>message</u> test: Determine whether the message:
   a. Does it express the will of God?
   b. Is it neutral, i.e., reflective of normal life?
   c. Is it against Christian standards or behavior?

Slide 31 of 96

2. The <u>association</u> test: Does the music identify with things, actions, or people that are contrary to Christianity? "Come out from among them and be separate, says the Lord" (2 Cor. 6:17).

3. The <u>memory</u> test: Does the music bring back things in your past that you have left? "Forgetting the things which are behind" (Phil. 3:13).

4. The <u>emotions</u> test: Does the music stir negative or lustful feelings within you?

Slide 32 of 96

5. The <u>purpose</u> test: Determine whether the music is sad, joyful, uplifting, soothing, etc.

6. The <u>understanding</u> test: Should you use music you don't understand or to which you cannot find the melody? Sometimes you need music appreciation for the classics or cultural explanation for music from other cultures.

7. The <u>musical</u> test: Does it have the "song within the song?" It has meaning to you without analysis.

Slide 33 of 96

Slide 34 of 96

Lesson 4

Alcohol: Can We Drink?

A. Introduction

Should alcoholic products like tobacco products be banned from television advertisements?

1. <u>Alcohol</u> is the greatest drug problem, not crack, meth, marijuana, etc.
2. <u>Finish strong</u>. It is impossible for the young man to start right. "In the days of Noah, they were . . . eating and drinking" (Matt. 24:37-38). But later in life after the flood, "He (Noah) drank of the wine and was drunken" (Gen. 9:21).
3. When a pregnant woman gets drunk, so does her baby. Fifty-two percent of all alcoholics had <u>alcoholic parents</u>.

Slide 35 of 96

B. Why I Am Against Liquor

What are the primary reasons for not drinking alcohol products?

1. God <u>rejects</u> drunkenness. Be not drunk with wine wherein is excess but be filled with the Sprit" (Eph. 5:18). "Do not look on the wine when it is red, when it sparkles in the cup" (Prov. 23:31). "Their wine is the poison" (Deut. 32:33). "Woe to him who gives drink to his neighbor, pressing him to your bottle" (Hab. 2:15). "Let us walk honestly, as in the day; not in rioting and drunkenness" (Rom. 13:13). "Nor drunkards shall inherit the kingdom of God" (1 Cor. 6:10).

Slide 36 of 96

2. Drunkenness destroys the <u>body</u>. "Your body is the temple of the Holy Spirit" (1 cor. 6:19). Whatever harms God's temple is wrong.

3. Drunkenness destroys <u>morals and integrity</u> of people. Statistical link between drunkenness and crime, i.e., not those who are guilty of drunkenness will commit crime, but those who commit crimes will probably drink excessively.

Slide 37 of 96

4. Drunkenness destroys <u>self-control</u> of people.
   a. "The fruit of the Spirit is . . . self-control" (Gal. 5:23). The word *temperance* that characterized the anti-drunkenness movement means "self-control."
   b. "Be temperate (self-controlled) in all things" (1 Cor. 9:25).
   c. The Bible does not use the term alcoholics (medical term), but drunkards (moral term).

Slide 38 of 96

5. Drunkenness is contrary to the <u>example of Christ</u>. "Christ . . . an example, that we should follow His steps" (1 Peter 2:21).

6. Alcohol is <u>addictive</u>.
   a. Alcohol is an anesthetic to kill pain and tranquilize.
   b. Alcohol makes a person dependent. One in eight heavy drinkers becomes an alcoholic (1) Psychological compulsive, (2) Sociological compulsive, and (3) Physical compulsive.

Slide 39 of 96

C. Two Kinds of Wine

Should a Christian drink non-alcoholic beer?

1. <u>Strong</u> wine – "violence" (Prov. 23:29-30); "venomous poison" (Prov. 23:31); "sick with wine" (Hosea 7:5); "cup of fury" (Jer. 25:15).

Slide 40 of 96

2. <u>Good</u> wine – "best" (Num. 18;12), "sweet savor" (Neh. 10:37); "new wine" (Neh. 10:39); "wine of prosperity" (Gen. 27:28; Deut. 11:14); "cheers" (Judges 9:13); "makes glad" (Ps. 104:14-15). The purpose of good wine:
   a. Offering to God (Num. 18;12).
   b. Quenches the thirst (Gen. 27:28).
   c. Symbol of prosperity and the Holy Spirit (Prov. 34:15; Judges 9:13; Prov. 9:2; Eph. 5:17).

Slide 41 of 96

4. Leaven <u>prohibited</u> (usually rotting skins, i.e., yeast).
   a. Leaven was a sign of <u>sin</u> (Matt. 13:33).
   b. Leaven was prohibited for six days before the <u>Passover</u> (Ex. 12:8; 15-20; 13:6-7).

Slide 43 of 96

2. Jesus created intoxicating wine at the wedding in Canna because they kept "the good wine until now" (John 2:11).
   a. <u>Social</u> argument – family affair would prohibit strong drink.
   b. <u>Process</u> argument -- juice comes from the clouds into the earth up through the vine, but Christ speeded the process instantaneously. Fermentation is a human additive; Christ used the process of nature.
   c. <u>Command</u> argument – "Do not look on the wine when it is red, when it swirls around smoothly" (Prov. 23:31).

Slide 45 of 96

E. How To Be Sober Life-Long

What would you tell a new Christian about alcohol?

1. <u>Know</u> – right thinking produces right action, i.e., realize that strong drink is prohibited in Scriptures.

2. Be <u>fearful</u>. No one knows if they are addicted.

3. Follow the <u>example</u> of Christ.

Slide 47 of 96

3. The difference was <u>fermentation</u>. "Fermentation is the result of the natural interaction of yeast (leaven) with the sugars and acid of the juice. As the liquid ferments in the presence of the grape skins . . . each passing hour in flavor, in color, in aroma, and in body which the winemaker monitors constantly. Fermentation causes heat (70 degrees), and the skins form a cap to produce body. When the right taste is reached, the temperature is reduced to stop fermentation." ~Ernest and Julio Gallo.

Slide 42 of 96

D. Did Jesus Condone Wine Drinking?

1. Jesus served intoxicating wine at the Last Supper . If Jesus served wine that was slightly intoxicating, it opens the door for beer or social drinking today.
   a. <u>Preparation</u> argument – leaven strictly prohibited during Passover week.
   b. <u>Command</u> argument – "Woe to him who gives drink to his neighbor" (Hab. 2:15).
   c. <u>Implicit</u> argument – it is never called wine but the cup or fruit of the vine.

Slide 44 of 96

3. The enemies claim, "The Son of Man came eating and drinking, and they say, 'Look, a glutton and a winebibber'" (Matt. 11:19).
   a. This is from His <u>enemies</u>. "Then the Jews answered and said to Him, 'Do we not say rightly that You are a Samaritan and have a demon?'" (John 8:48).
   b. This is a <u>comparison</u> with John the Baptist who was a Nazarite, i.e., no sweet wine.

Slide 46 of 96

4. Make a <u>commitment</u> to your future/present spouse of an "alcohol free" home.

5. <u>Promise</u> yourself you will never take your first or another drink of alcohol.

6. Be <u>careful</u> of alcohol influenced attractions, i.e., cooking with it, alcohol-free beer, etc.

7. <u>Bend over backwards</u> when in an alcohol environment, "Avoid the appearance of evil (1 Thess. 5:22).

Slide 48 of 96

Lesson 5

Language

A. Introduction

As America becomes more secular, she also becomes more hostile to Christianity. No negative influences are more evident of this attack than the filthy speech movement, including profanity and blasphemy.

B. Definition

1. Swearing – to utter and oath or declaration with an appeal to God or a sacred object; to direct judgment for mere emphasis.

2. Cursing – to ask God to bring harm or evil to a person or object; to speak blasphemy. A curse carries its own power of execution. The opposite of "to bless."

3. Blasphemy – to direct curses or judgment toward God or His sacred object.

4. Filthy language – morally vile or obscene language toward parts of the body to convey the idea of disgust.

5. Profanity – bridges the gap between swearing and filthy language. To show utter disregard for God.

6. Slang – language markedly colloquial, regarding the standards of cultural speech, having meaning to those within the "in group."

C. Observations From Life

1. Swearing no longer dominates only boys.

2. One out of 14 college student's words are swear words.

3. Upper class groups are least likely to swear.

4. Research – children tend to swear from hearing their parents swear.

5. American civil Liberties Union (ACLU) has successfully challenged laws dealing with profanity.

D. Biblical Observations

1. "You shall not take the name of the Lord your God in vain, for the Lord will not hold him guiltless who takes His name in vain" (Ex. 20:7).
   a. Vain – to waste, disorder, empty, or to use God's name for lying or false swearing.
   b. Guiltless – allow to go unpunished.

2. Blasphemy – punishable by stoning (Lev. 24:10-16).

3. "Michael the archangel, in contending with the devil, when he disputed about the body of Moses, dared not bring against him a reviling accusation, but said, 'The Lord rebuke you!'" (Jude 9).

4. Peter – " Then he began to call down curses, and he swore to them" (Matt. 26:74, *NIV*).

5. Jesus – "Bless them which curse you" (Luke 6:24).

6. Paul – "Neither filthiness nor foolish talking" (Eph. 5:4).

7. "But now you yourselves are to put off all these: anger, wrath, malice, blasphemy, filthy language out of your mouth" (Col. 3:8).

E. Why People Use Wrong Language

1. Stirring up authorities quoted in *Time Magazine*. It is motivated by:
   a. Rebellion against restraints.
   b. Desire for freedom or independence.

2. Expression of anger. The deeper the rage, the more vicious the language.

3. Equalize – a tool of feminism to demonstrate equalization between men and women, quoted in *Time Magazine*.

4. Flaunt superiority – it is considered a statement.

5. Habit – it represents sub-verbal urges or is the result of modeling by an adult role mode.

6. Rebellion against God. "But those things which proceed out of the mouth come from the heart, and they defile a man. For out of the heart proceed evil thoughts, murders, adulteries, fornications, thefts, false witness, blasphemies" (Matt. 15:18-19).

Slide 57 of 96

4. Avoid striving for acceptance among the unchurched by suing their words, symbols, and speech patterns.

5. Realize wrong language will interfere with your growth in Christ and testimony to the world.

6. Remember all your speech reflects your inner person.

Slide 59 of 96

10. Don't separate from cursers but avoid their language and be a wholesome testimony. "Let no corrupt word proceed out of your mouth, but what is good for necessary [a]edification, that it may impart grace to the hearers" (Eph. 4:29).

11. Be careful. "Let your speech be always with grace, seasoned with salt, that you may know how to answer every man" (Col. 4:6).

Slide 61 of 96

Lesson 6

Dancing

Slide 63 of 96

F. Twelve Steps To Proper Speech

1. A believer must realize his or her language is wrong. Until there is motivation against a bad habit, there is no motivation toward a good habit.

2. Even though some words have evolved into acceptance by society, the Christian should not lead in their use.

3. Try to be proper in all things. Learn and use words properly according to God's Word and culture.

Slide 58 of 96

7. Pick out a Christian role model to follow in all things. Paul said, "Be followers of me, even as I also am of Christ" (1 Cor. 11:1). "The things which you learned and received and heard (Paul had good language) and saw in me, these do" (Phil. 4:9).

8. Stop watching bad movies and television shows.

9. Get smart. "Bad language is a dead giver away that the user is showing their ignorance" ~*Saturday Review*.

Slide 60 of 96

12. Memorize and mediate on Scriptures. "Let the word of Christ dwell in you richly in all wisdom, teaching and admonishing one another in psalms and hymns and spiritual songs, singing with grace in your hearts to the Lord. And whatever you do in word or deed, do all in the name of the Lord Jesus, giving thanks to God the Father through Him" (Col. 3:16-17).

Slide 62 of 96

A. Introduction

1. Definition: "A series of rhythmic and patterned bodily movements performed to music." ~Webster

2. Biblical dances – An emotional and physical expression of the entire body in rhythmic movement to music for a specific purpose. "Then David danced before the Lord" (2 Sam. 6:14).
   a. What is your purpose? David danced to God.
   b. What are you expressing? Praise and gratitude.
   c. How are you moving? Positive feelings before God.

Slide 64 of 96

3. In the 50s hugging; in the 70s separate; in the 90s (Madonna and Michael Jackson) alone.

B. Unacceptable Dancing In The Bible

1. Rebellion. "He saw the calf and the dancing. So, Moses' anger became hot, and he cast the tablets out of his hands and broke them at the foot of the mountain" (Ex. 32:19).

2. Seduction. "When Herodias' daughter . . . came in and danced, and pleased Herod and those who sat with him" (Mark 6:22).

Slide 65 of 96

D. Test For Dancing

1. The following tests should be applied to situations that involve dancing. The thought test. The greatest appeal of Christianity is to the mind or the appeal of truth. We are thinking people made in the image of a rational God. What you think is imperative. Ask, "what are you thinking when you participate in this dance?" "Whatsoever things are true . . . honest . . . just . . . pure . . . lovely . . . good report, if there be any virtue, if there be any praise, think on these things" (Phil. 14:8).

Slide 67 of 96

4. The association test. Ask yourself, "should I be around the people I am dancing with?" "Should I be dancing with this person?" "Should I be associated with the music's artist?"

5. The place test. You have to ask, "Should I be in the place where I am dancing?" This may or may not be a physical place, but a circumstance. "Do you not know that friendship with the world is enmity with God?" (James 4:4). While a place is not evil, what is evil is the believer's support of evil in that place and the believer's identification with evil in a place. Jesus explained, "I do not pray that You should take them out of the world, but that You should keep them from the evil one" (John 17:15).

Slide 69 of 96

Lesson 7

Lies

Slide 71 of 96

C. Acceptable Dancing In The Bible

1. Expression of praise. "Let them praise His name in the dance" (Ps. 149:3, 150:4).
2. Sometimes acceptable. "A time to weep, a time to laugh; a time to mourn, a time to dance" (Ecc. 3:4). Dancing associated with joyful emotions.
3. Acceptable description. "We have piped unto you and ye have not danced"(Matt. 11:17).
4. Symbol of happiness. "Thou hast turned for me my mourning into dancing" (Ps. 20:11).

Slide 66 of 96

2. The message test. All music makes a statement. Ask, "what is being said by the words and music?"

3. The desire test. Ask yourself, "what does this dance do to my desires? Two more questions flow out of the first. "Does this dance arouse my lust toward my partner or someone else?" Second, "does this dancing lower my resistance so that I may participate in other lustful dancing or other harmful activities?" "But each one is tempted when he is drawn away by his own desires and enticed. Then, when desire has conceived, it gives birth to sin; and sin, when it is full-grown, brings forth death" (James 1:14-15).

Slide 68 of 96

6. The testimony test Ask, "What will my dancing do to other people?" Your freedom may harm another. "But beware lest somehow this liberty of yours become a stumbling block to those who are weak" (1 Cor. 8:9).

7. The music test. All music has "the song within the song." Is this good music or poor music?

Slide 70 of 96

A. Introduction

1. Root and fruit. No one teaches small children to lie. You lie because you have a lying nature, not because you became a liar, but because you told an untruth. All men are liars (Ps. 116:11).

2. Those who lie make it twice on God's list. "Six things the Lord hates, yes, seven are an abomination to Him . . . (1) a lying tongue . . . (2) a false witness who speaks lies" (Prov. 6:16-19).

Slide 72 of 96

B. Three Definitions of Lying

1. <u>Active</u>. "To make an untrue statement with the intent to deceive." ~Webster

2. <u>Passive</u>. To create a false, or misleading impression.

3. <u>Inner</u>. To tolerate internal compromise with what you know is right.

Slide 73 of 96

C. Four Steps of A Lie

1. To <u>create</u> deceit. You begin to calculate or make-up a life.

2. To relay <u>dishonesty</u>. You communicate to another something that is not truth, i.e., a lie.

3. <u>Intend</u> to mislead or misrepresent.

4. Avoid moral <u>responsibly</u>. A lie is conspiracy participating in a cover up or falsehood. But those who do so, know what they do and are responsible to themselves and to God.

Slide 74 of 96

D. Judging The Types of Lies

1. <u>White</u> lies. Telling an untruth to deceive, but for a good purpose.

2. <u>Political</u> lies. Telling an untruth to flatter or not telling the truth to keep from embarrassing someone.

3. <u>Gossip</u> lies. To tell what should not be told with a selfish purpose.

Slide 75 of 96

4. <u>Sinister</u> lies. To seek to hear things that are not true and pass them on to harm another.

5. <u>Jovial</u> lies. An obvious untruth to all for the purpose of humor and enjoyment.

6. <u>Half</u> lies. To not tell al with the intent to deceive.

7. <u>Excuses</u> lies. To give reason or explanation that may or may not be the primary cause.

Slide 76 of 96

8. <u>Hypocrisy</u> lies to claim to be something that is contrary to your life.

9. <u>Justifying</u> lies. If I lie about my numbers, and you know that I lied, and I know you know that I lied, isn't that like telling the truth.

10. <u>Face-saying</u> lies. "Sarah laughed within herself" (Gen. 1:12). "The Lord said, 'wherefore did Sarah laugh?'" (v. 13). "Sarah denied . . . 'I laughed not'" (v. 15).

Slide 77 of 96

11. <u>Evangelistic</u> lies. "Peter said to Ananias, 'Ananias, why has Satan filled your heart to lie to the Holy Spirit?'" (Acts 5:3). Theoretically, you cannot lie to God because He knows everything.

12. <u>Propaganda</u> lies. You give your side of the truth but ignore or hide the other side.

13. <u>Advertisement</u> lies. Persuading people of the benefits not considering the limitations or qualifications.

Slide 78 of 96

14. <u>Cheating</u> lies. To claim something that does not belong to you.

15. <u>Demonic</u> lies. When you call truth a lie, and you present a lie as truth. "Send them strong delusion, that they should believe the lie" (2 Thess. 2:11). "Who exchanged the truth of God for the lie" (Rom. 1:25).

16. Put a <u>spin</u> on the truth. You tell a negative story in a way that makes you look good.

Slide 79 of 96

E. How To Overcome The Habit of Lying

1. Look to the <u>standard</u>. "I am the . . . truth" (Jesus).

2. Realize the <u>source</u> of lying. You are of your father the devil . . . he is a liar" (John 8:44).

3. Admit your <u>nature</u> is deceitful. "The heart is deceitful and desperately wicked" (Jer. 17:9). "For out of the heart proceeds evil thoughts . . . false witness" (Matt. 15:19).

Slide 80 of 96

4. Recognize the <u>fate</u> of liars. "But the fearful and unbelievers . . . and all liars shall have their part in the lake which burns with fire" (Rev. 21:8).

5. Respond to your <u>obligation</u>. "Therefore, putting away lying, 'Let each one of you speak truth with his neighbor,' for we are members of one another" (Eph. 4:25).

6. Determine to be a <u>radical</u> disciple. "If anyone desires to come after Me, let him deny himself, and take up his cross daily, and follow Me" (Luke 9:23).

7. Walk in <u>forgiveness</u>. God knows "all men are liars" but in mercy forgives all. "They (Israel) lied to Him (God) with their tongues . . . but He being full of compassion, forgave their iniquity" (Ps. 78:36-38).

8. Ask for <u>strength</u>. "Our Father . . . forgive us our debts" (Matt. 6:9-12).

9. Make a <u>decision</u> to tell the truth. There is power in a simple decision made by the total person.

10. Resolve to be a person of <u>character</u>. The worst thing I life is to allow internal compromise.

   a. Others cannot trust you if you don't trust yourself.
   b. If your self-wroth deteriorates, you cannot direct yourself.

Lesson 8

Racism

A. Introduction

1. Definition:
   a. <u>Discriminate</u>. "To make a difference in treatment or favor on a basis rather than merit" ~Webster.
   b. <u>Racism</u> – "Belief that racial difference produces an inherent superiority of a particular race" ~Webster.
   c. Synonyms for race – nations, Gentiles, ethnic groups, people groups, family, class, tribe.

2. First mention. "The Gentiles were divided in their lands, everyone by his tongue, after their families in their nations" (Gen. 10:5). "I will make of thee (Abraham) a great nation" (Gen. 12:2).

3. Biological <u>source</u>. Why are there different races?
   a. <u>Creation</u>, but God created only two, Adam and Eve. All others come from some source.
   b. <u>Environment</u>. The sun made the Africans black and the Scandinavians blond-haired and washed skin. But the original genetics do not return when environment changes.
   c. Embryonic difference were innate in first created person. "Adam is the head of the human race." And environmental differences were reinforced by environment, sovereignly assigned by God.

4. Theological <u>source</u>. God made us different. "When the Most High divided the nations (races) their inheritance . . . He set the bounds of the people according to the number of the children of Israel"(Deut. 32:9). The number of races ahs something to do with Jews.

5. Why different in races?
   a. Every person is made in the image of God. "Let Us make man in Our image after Our likeness" (Gen. 1:26). But no one person <u>perfectly reflects</u> God. The great intellectual person reflects God's mind, and the deeply emotional mother reflects God's love. We understand God's love from a broader perspective of various people.

b. Every race reflects a <u>different</u> aspect of God. The self-disciplined oriental, the entrepreneurial driven Anglo, or the hospitable Egyptian. You must see all races to get a broad view of God.

c. Since God made us all like Himself, it is <u>anti-faith</u> to dislike one race, for you deny the purpose and nature of God.

Slide 89 of 96

6. Priority of <u>evangelism</u>. Jesus commanded to plant churches for all races, "Go therefore and make disciples of all races" (Matt. 28;19). Jesus commanded to evangelize every person, "Go . . . preach the Gospel to every creature"(Matt. 16:15).

7. Races in <u>Heaven</u>. You will keep your racial characteristics in Heaven. "The leaves of the tree were for the healing (growth) of the races" (Rev. 22:2). "They sang a new song . . . You . . . have redeemed us to God by Your blood out of every tribe and tongue and people and nation" (Rev. 5:9). "I beheld a great multitude . . . of all nations (races) and kindred, and people, and tongues"(Rev. 7:9).

Slide 90 of 96

B. Problem of Growing Racism/Violence

Depression Kids	Baby Boomers	Busters
1925-1945	1945-1965	1965-1985
Last segregated	Integrated	Racist
War mentality	Idealistic	Violent
Won WWII	Hated Vietnam	Wins Vietnam
Conservative	Optimistic	Pessimistic

Slide 91 of 96

1. The five steps of racism:
   a. <u>Inward</u> – you value your race as superior based on racial differences to another.
   b. <u>Outward</u> – you devalue another person with less value.
   c. <u>Expression</u> – you act, decide, express opinions or make outward actions to them.
   d. <u>Results</u> – to the detriment of that race, yourself, and your race.
   e. <u>Compromises</u> your relationship with God.

2. Trend: <u>increased</u> racism and violence in spite of Boomer song, *"I liked to teach the world to sing in perfect harmony."*

Slide 92 of 96

3. Why? Race relations prosper when righteous laws are enforced equally to the benefit of all.
   a. Law subdues ancient <u>hatred</u>.
   b. Decline in the influence of Christianity.
   c. Blindness to needs of some.
   d. Ineffectiveness or unbalanced media.
   e. <u>Pride</u> (ethnocentrism).
   f. Fear.
   g. <u>Ignorance</u>.
   h. Ethnic cleansing.
   i. Holocaust.
   j. Politically correct.

Slide 93 of 96

C. Answers To Racism

1. <u>Command</u>. "We should love one another" (1 John 2:11).

2. Example of <u>Christ</u>. "How is it that You, being a Jew, ask a drink from me, a Samaritan woman?" (John 4:9).

3. Cross-cultural <u>evangelism</u>. Never compromise biblical doctrine or enteral principles but adapt methods to reach people where they are and lift them to where they should be.

Slide 94 of 96

4. <u>Regeneration</u>. "Can anyone forbid water, that these should not be baptized who have received the Holy Spirit just as we have?" (Acts 10:47).

5. New <u>position</u>. "There is neither Greek nor Jew, circumcised nor uncircumcised, barbarian, Scythian, slave nor free, but Christ is all and in all" (Col. 3:11). "There is neither Jew nor Greek . . . neither male nor female; for you are all one in Christ Jesus." (Gal. 3:28).

6. Give to others but demand nothing for <u>yourself</u>.

Slide 95 of 96

7. Remember a race <u>less fortunate</u> than yours. Instead of always protecting your race, focus on those less fortunate than your race.

8. Ask for <u>color blind</u> eyes. Some races have an advantage over your race, just as yours has advantages.

9. We all have the same <u>human</u> characteristic.

Slide 96 of 96

PART FOUR

WHAT IS RIGHT?

ADDITIONAL RESOURCES

POWERPOINT SLIDES:

To purchase and download the Powerpoint Slides go to
https://www.norimediagroup.com/pages/elmer-towns

VIDEO:

To purchase available video by Dr Towns go to
https://www.norimediagroup.com/pages/elmer-towns

ADD-ON CONTENT

To purchase additional products in this series go to
https://www.norimediagroup.com/pages/elmer-towns

RELATED BOOKS

Available at https://www.norimediagroup.com/pages/elmer-towns